CW01020144

Contents

Author's Note

Dr Charles Margerison is a Chartered Psychologist, a member of the Royal Institution and the Royal Literature Society. He is Chairman of Viewpoint Resources Ltd, a publishing organisation. Previously, he was Professor of Management at the University of Cranfield, UK and also at the University of Queensland, Australia.

The author of more than ten books on management issues, he has written an innovative continuing professional development system, called *The Communication and Problem Solving Resource*. He is the co-founder of Team Management Systems and the Chairman of Bell Hughes Music Group. He lives in Queensland, Australia.

Dr Margerison is the founder and author of the Amazing People Club Series. This unique range is based on BioViews®, a new concept that combines a biography with a virtual interview. The stories are presented as if written by the amazing people concerned and are an interpretation of their lives, as in a theatre play. BioViews® offer new and interesting ways of understanding major contributions to our world. The stories are inspirational and can help you achieve your ambitions in your own journey through life.

Thanks to Frances Corcoran, Katharine Smith, Kirri Robinson, James Maxwell, Emily Hamilton, Dennis Bedson, Emma Braithwaite, Alan Earnst, Monica Lawlor and Rodney Bain for their great work on the production of this book.

Introduction

Today, more and more women become doctors, politicians, entrepreneurs, scientists, financial advisers, and take on other roles outside the home. This, of course, has certainly not always been the case.

The women in this book were trailblazers. Their stories are a source of inspiration and are revealed through our BioView® format. A BioView® is a unique new story format. Each story is a biography, written as a virtual interview, to reflect the life story of an amazing person. BioViews® offer interesting and easy ways to learn from those who have made major contributions to our world. BioViews® are inspirational stories that can help you achieve your ambitions on life's journey. You can discover how these amazing women lived, loved and worked in their own distinct ways. For example:

- Elizabeth Blackwell became the first qualified female doctor in the USA, and the first woman to be registered as a doctor in England.

- Golda Meir was born in the Ukraine, educated in America, and became the first female Prime Minister of Israel.

- Marie Curie moved from Poland to France where she studied Science and went on to win two Nobel Prizes.

- Sally Hemings was a slave in America who went to work for her owner in France, where she developed an amazing relationship with him that shaped the rest of her life.

- Edith Piaf lost her eyesight when a child, but regained it and started singing on the streets to commence her outstanding career.

We can learn key lessons from each one of them. In particular, their achievements were the result of their determination to continue on, regardless of how difficult the journey. They believed in what they had to offer, and used their time well.

I trust that you will find the book informative as well as enjoyable.

Dr Charles Margerison

Nancy Astor
1879–1964

Until 1919, all Members of the British Parliament were men
That is when I disturbed their peace
Two things in particular disturbed them
Firstly, I was the first woman to take a seat in Parliament
Of equal concern was that I was American
To many Members of Parliament, this added insult to injury
How dare a woman from one of the old colonies return to taunt them?
If a woman had to be allowed in, why not an English woman?
This was the atmosphere surrounding my win at Plymouth Sutton
For years and years, Parliament had debated giving women the vote
There was more talk than action until the suffragettes took to the streets
Only in 1918 did women over 30 years of age get the vote
Ironically, the first woman elected to Parliament was not a suffragette
Nor was I the first to be elected
Countess de Markievicz, the Irish patriot, had that honour
It was an honour that she did not accept
She was a member of Sinn Fein, the Irish liberation movement
Although elected, she refused on principle to take her seat in Parliament
It would have been difficult anyway, as she was in prison
She was captured during the Easter Rising of 1916 in Dublin
Therefore, the first woman elected to Parliament was a convict
I was born in Virginia, the first British Colony in America
One of five sisters, known as the Gibson Girls
My parents called me Nancy Witcher Langhorne
We were raised in the privileged surroundings of a rich family
Therefore, I had an American accent and colonial heritage
Many members of the House reflected on the irony
I was too busy to worry about the past
It had not been pleasant to me
My first marriage was to Robert Shaw in 1897
It was not a good choice, though it did result in the birth of my first son
We divorced in 1903 and I left the USA
Mainly due to my husband's drinking problem
Arriving in England, I settled into a new single lifestyle

Nancy Astor

In 1906, I met and married Waldorf Astor
Born in the USA, on the same day as me
He was attractive and came from a rich family
Also, he was a Member of Parliament for Plymouth Sutton
In 1919, he succeeded to the peerage and joined the House of Lords
To do this, he had to renounce his elected position
We agreed that I should stand for election to take his place
The good people of Plymouth Sutton agreed and elected me
The majority felt I would do the job well, American or not
So, that is what I did from 1919 to 1945
It was a tremendous responsibility and challenge

Cliveden House

The rights of women and children were my key concerns
Debate was in Parliament, decisions were usually made elsewhere
Often, the real politics took place in the clubs around London
Most of the clubs were not open to women
Fortunately, I was able to establish my own select club
My father-in-law gave my husband and I a fantastic wedding gift
It was called Cliveden, a beautiful mansion in Buckinghamshire
We invited influential guests, as well as friends
Winston Churchill, James Balfour and Rudyard Kipling were just three
Naturally, we mixed business with pleasure and discussed politics
It was also the centre of our family life
In addition, we had a substantial home in St James's Square, London

Ironically, it became one of the major London clubs
For us, it was a home and political centre of influence
We had six children and they grew up understanding the key issues
In all, with family, politics and social meetings, it was a busy life
Also, travel to and from the constituency and Cliveden took time
Throughout, my husband supported my aspirations
Only when the last of my children was born did I enter Parliament
Aged 40, I had a wide understanding of people's needs and the issues
For years, I had visited Plymouth to help my husband in his work
Many people knew me
Some were nonetheless shocked by my decision
Standing for the Conservative Party against two male candidates
Fortunately, I had a gift for public speaking
Lloyd George told me, 'Your voice is your fortune'
A compliment indeed from such a fine orator
My sayings became known as 'Astorisms'
I said what I felt, without fear or favour
Sometimes it was a serious point and sometimes a funny point
I pressed for better primary education and a curb on drinking
Action at the local level was especially required
Maternity centres and crèches were therefore established
Improved housing was another focus point
There was so much to do, particularly after 1929
The years of the depression hit my constituents hard
Likewise, so did the years of the World Wars
During that time, we established a hospital at Cliveden
It helped many soldiers to recover and recuperate
Throughout, I was guided by my strong beliefs
Having seen the evil that alcohol could bring, I said so
Having seen the problems with Communism, I spoke against it
My religious views were also well-known
With Philip Kerr, I supported the Christian Science religion
Previously, I had been a Catholic
In speaking my mind, I annoyed various groups
That is the nature of politics and religion
It was also the essence of free speech
As the first lady to take a seat in Parliament, I welcomed that freedom
May other women do likewise.

Elizabeth Blackwell
1821–1910

Crossing the Atlantic in 1832 was a great experience
The waves raged against the side of our boat
As an 11 year old, I enjoyed it, though others felt ill
The experience reflected the future of my life
Riding the waves of anger and opposition
For I decided that my life would be devoted to helping others
My father was opening a new sugar refining venture in Ohio, USA
Our family of nine was sailing to a new land and new life
Born in Bristol, England, we were moving from the city to the country
Father was a Quaker and had all my brothers and sisters educated
The process helped me think about my aims and aspirations
It provided me with an objective, something to engross my thoughts
Helping others could prevent the sad wearing away of the heart
When finishing school, I did not just want to be married off
It was important to make a difference
Particularly, as I saw my father taking ill and dying
When I suggested that I become a doctor, it was seen as silly
That was work for men, I was told
Through contacts, I arranged to work with Dr S. Dickson
Living at his home in South Carolina, he tutored me in medicine
The problem was how to gain a University qualification
Writing letter after letter, I waited eagerly for the responses
17 medical schools rejected my applications
Some did not give a reason, others were very clear
Medical education was reserved for men
Those who replied said it was not a job for a lady
Dealing with disease and surgery was men's work, they said
Eventually, I wrote to the Faculty at Geneva College, New York
The staff were no doubt amused that a girl had applied
They sent the application to the students, to allow them to decide
Fortunately, they voted for me, despite opposition from the faculty
The education course was far easier than gaining entry
In 1849, I graduated as head of the class, two years after starting
So becoming the first woman to qualify as a medical doctor in the USA

Elizabeth Blackwell

En route, there was prejudice and some bizarre incidents
One of the surgery classes was on male organs
The tutor in charge asked me not to attend
Maybe to spare my blushes, or restrict my education
I offered to remove my bonnet and attended
Qualifying as a doctor did not mean I could gain work
Most hospitals barred me because I was a female
Therefore, I decided to train in a subject helpful to women
My decision was to go to France and become a midwife
There, I studied at La Maternité, the children's hospital
Treating a child with an eye infection, I contracted purulent opthalmia
It spread dangerously and surgeons had to remove one of my eyes
That cut short my training and stay in Paris
I went to England and worked in London with Dr Puget
Establishing links that would, in due course, develop further
Returning to America in 1851, I resolved to work with children
In the process, I was able to help many mothers
Indeed, although not married, I became a mother by adoption
Katherine Barry was a three year old orphan and in need of help
It was the least that I could do and she brought joy to my life
Kitty, as she became known, was my lifelong companion
With the passing of the years, she helped me, as I had helped her
Medical facilities for women and children were poor
Hospitals and pharmacies still refused to employ women
Therefore, I purchased a house in New York to set up a clinic
Even then, women were reluctant to visit a woman doctor
In 1852, I therefore wrote a book
The Laws of Life
With Special Reference to the Physical Education of Girls
It was a small start to improve the health of females
At that time, they were not supposed to talk about their bodies
As a result, many illnesses went undetected
Taking the clinic to the slums of New York was vital
The need was greatest there, with so many people and so few doctors
In 1853, with some help from friends, a small dispensary was set up
The people who came to visit were most thankful
It encouraged me to continue
Our medical work was combined with social work

The focus on education and hygiene was a vital part of social medicine
That was in contrast to the focus other doctors had on surgery
In 1857, I established a new type of hospital
The New York Infirmary for Indigent Women and Children
It was a small start for a large and growing problem area
Eventually, the United States Sanitary Commission was established
It was based in many ways on the work we did in the New York slums
News of my work spread to Britain and a lecture tour took place in 1859
As a result, I became the first woman on the British Medical Register

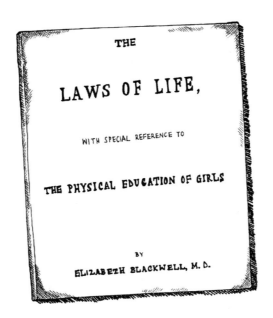

THE

LAWS OF LIFE,

WITH SPECIAL REFERENCE TO

THE PHYSICAL EDUCATION OF GIRLS

BY

ELIZABETH BLACKWELL, M. D.

But, ironically, women were not allowed to qualify as doctors there
More prejudice in the land of my birth
On my return to the USA, the Civil War commenced
To assist, I trained nurses to tend injured soldiers
It was a sad time, with nearly 1,000,000 casualties
Two-thirds of those were due to disease, rather than battle wounds
The Women's Central Association of Relief was also established
After the war, most hospitals refused to hire me
In 1868, I therefore set up an organisation to resolve the problem

The Women's Medical College of the New York Infirmary
The name made a clear statement of intent
My sister, Emily, and Dr Marie Zakrzews joined me
It was a precursor to similar work in England
Friends, like Elizabeth Garrett, promoted women's rights
Setting sail to the land of my birth again, I resolved to assist
The boat bravely rode the waves, reminding me of my early days
During the voyage, I made a plan of what to do
In 1869, I helped form the National Health Society in England
With an influential group of women, we made a start
The London School of Medicine for Women was also established
As Professor of Gynaecology from 1875 to 1907, I helped mothers
By 1899, we had trained 364 women doctors
Despite this, there was continued opposition to women doctors
It was vital to convince politicians that changes were needed
Influencing those with power could provide more resources
In 1876, Parliament agreed to register doctors, regardless of gender
It was an important milestone
Writing and tutoring were equally important
My book, *The Moral Education of the Young*, was published
Also, I wrote to help women become professionals
Pioneer Work In Opening the Medical Profession to Women
That was the title I gave to my autobiography
My parents would have approved
But, more needed to be done through social medicine
Most homes were basic and in need of repair
In England and America, people crowded into the cities
The social conditions were the cause of much disease
In the USA, slavery was the red hot political issue
I campaigned with others to have slavery abolished
Poverty and city slums were key issues
On my return to America, I campaigned to make improvements
Better housing and food could cure many ailments
Beliefs and principles were important to me
Periods of time were spent as an Episcopalian
Then, I became a Dissenter, and later a Unitarian
Eventually, I joined the Christian Socialist group
Seeking not only a church but a community of activists

Prayer by itself was not enough
Practical action to bring about social change was needed
Doctors focused more on curing illness
Hygiene and prevention was more of a priority for me
Helping educate women on how to manage their families' health
These were the issues that touched my heart
Some say I was married to my work
Maybe so, for the cause was worth it.

Edith Cavell
1865–1915

I broke a law, but I was not a criminal
It was a German military law, and I disagreed with it
At the time, I was a nurse working in a Belgian hospital
The First World War was raging all around us
The Germans took over the hospital
From that point on, my life was in danger
In addition to caring for soldiers, I helped them to avoid capture
The penalty for helping soldiers escape was death
I was a long way from where I was born in Swardeston, Norfolk
My family had strong religious and humanitarian values
Each day, I was reminded of these
My father taught me the importance of helping others
Belief in God and the Ten Commandments were the simple rules
For 45 years, my father was the village vicar
It was a quiet place and, aged about 20, I went in search of a new world
At school, I did well at French and wanted to use it in my work
To gain international experience, I moved to Brussels
There, I worked as a governess and tutor for the Francois family
In 1895, my father became ill and I returned to nurse him
We discussed my work and career
Most girls of my age were married and were having children
Although I had some friendships, there was no prospect of marriage
What should I do?
I did not want to marry just to get a wedding ring
I realised that route would bring me unhappiness
Equally, some dull, repetitive job would have the same effect
However, I wanted to work where I was needed and there was a challenge
Father suggested that I could help many people by training as a nurse
When he died, the following year I decided to go on a training course
It was called The London Hospital Nurses Scheme
Upon qualifying, I gained valuable experience in hospitals
It was challenging work and I was both needed and appreciated
In 1901, I became the Night Supervisor at St Pancras Infirmary
Then, I moved to Shoreditch Infirmary

Edith Cavell

As a result of a meeting, I was asked to return to Belgium
Dr Antoine Depage had established a non-denominational nursing facility
That is how I joined the Berkendael Institute, near Brussels
Gradually, we built up a successful centre for training nurses
Life was once again quiet but still demanding
Devoted to my work, I had not married
In 1914, I returned home to have a holiday with my mother
The newspapers proclaimed that First World War had commenced
Action was needed to tend the wounded
As a nurse, I could contribute
Therefore, I volunteered for service with the Red Cross
The Berkendael Institute was converted to a hospital

Given my experience in Belgium, they asked me to return as the Matron
Soldiers of all ranks were sent there with terrible injuries
We worked hard to help them recover
Each day, more soldiers arrived
Their description of life at the battle front was horrific
Many suffered as much mentally as they did physically
They had seen sights that no one should see
Fighting hand to hand for their lives
Facing gas, as well as grenade weapons
Some felt guilty
Their comrades were still fighting, while they were in hospital
Surprising as it may seem, they wanted to return to the Front
That was a regular source of conversation and planning
In September 1914, Herman Capiau came to see me
He said some British soldiers were trapped behind enemy lines

They had been separated from their units
Sympathetic locals were hiding them, but the soldiers had to escape
If the Germans found them, they would be treated as spies
As a result, both the soldiers and the families would be shot
I agreed to house the soldiers, but there were risks
The Germans would say our organisation was harbouring spies
The first two soldiers were Dudley Boger and Frank Meachin
They were disguised as Belgian labourers
Once Herman Capiau returned home, he spread the word
Other escapees started to arrive
At one point, we had 35 of them in the building
Some injured soldiers wanted to escape to Holland
From there, they could make their way back to England
However, the Germans had captured Brussels on August 14th
Many of their troops were also injured
They were brought in and given nursing care
The German officers told me to convert the training unit into a hospital
More injured German soldiers began to arrive, plus our own troops
We soon had more than 200 British, German and French patients
As the Red Cross, we were honour-bound to help all victims
However, the Germans heard about some soldiers who had escaped
Colleagues warned me that the German officers were suspicious
On July 31st 1915, they arrested my colleague, Phillipe Baucq
Six days later, they returned and arrested me
After a period in solitary confinement, the Germans interviewed me
An officer said that he knew that I was helping British soldiers to escape
If I made a confession, he said he would spare my colleague's life
I told them what I knew
But, they did not honour their word and used the information against me
After nine frightening weeks in a dreadful prison, they put me on trial
It was a court martial open only to the German military
The trial only lasted two days
The German judge declared me guilty
He showed no mercy and I was sentenced to death
In the next few days, the British Government did little to help me
The Americans made vigorous protests
The Spanish Ambassador also protested, but it was all to no avail
The Rev. Stirling Gahan, an English Chaplain, came to see me

I told him that, "I know now that patriotism is not enough.
I must have no hatred towards anyone."
Saving lives was the most important thing for me
That is the work to which I had dedicated my life
He said that he would pray for my life
At dawn on October 12th 1915, I was put in front of a firing squad
Philippe Baucq had also been declared guilty and was there
I became light-headed and felt faint
The German soldiers were instructed to shoot me
In the silence, not in the heat of battle, they raised their guns
Preparing to conduct a cold-blooded murder.

Postscript

The British Government used Edith Cavell's death for propaganda
They wanted to introduce conscription
Her murder was used to further raise emotions
Yet, the Government had done little to assist her
Many monuments were created in her memory
Hospitals and schools were named after her
They reflected the values for which she stood.

EDITH CAVELL
BRUSSELS
DAWN
OCTOBER 12
1915
PATRIOTISM IS NOT ENOUGH
I MUST HAVE NO HATRED OR
BITTERNESS FOR ANYONE

Coco Chanel
1883–1971

Being born poor does not mean you have to stay poor
That was my philosophy in life
After all, we cannot choose our parents
In my case, my mother, Jeanne Devolle, had problems
I was her second illegitimate daughter
At the time of my birth, it was more than a talking point
The poorhouse at Saumur was my birthplace
My birth certificate read Gabrielle Chasnel
The local mayor was not too good at spelling
Eventually, my parents married
Maybe the social pressure in a small town got to them
Perhaps their circumstances had improved
It was a crowded house
With two sisters and three brothers, our home was always lively
Until that dreadful day, when mother died from tuberculosis
I was only 12 years old and lost for words
Father, who was a travelling salesman, left us
He could not cope with five small children
The nuns at the convent of Aubazine took us in
They were strict, but we survived because of their care
The experience enabled me to gain an education
Also, all the girls were taught how to be seamstresses
We were also expected to pray and lead the religious life
It was quiet, secluded and protected
Not like the world I had known
We only saw life outside the convent during school holidays
Then, we visited relatives who were kind to us
The nuns also taught me practical skills, like cooking
These came in useful when, at the age of 18, I left the convent
It was the start of an incredible life
My first job was in a tailor's shop
It was there that I found my talent for designing hats
These caught the attention of ladies, enabling me to earn extra money
It was my first step to financial independence

Coco Chanel

Yet, my attention was also drawn elsewhere
Etienne Balsan, a rich playboy, came into my life
He was three years older than me and had *savoir faire*
Born into a family of wealthy industrialists, he showed me a good time
I learnt how a girl from a poor background could live the high life
We became lovers, but both knew that we would not marry
We had many good times and he became a lifelong friend
Between 1905 and 1908, I was a singer in cafés and late night bars
It was suggested that I have a stage name

'Coco Chanel' was the name that I chose and it stayed with me
Ironically, it was to have more impact on the stage of *haute couture*
In due course, we separated and Arthur Capel became my lover
He was a rich and confident English officer friend of Etienne's
It was a long relationship from 1909 to 1918
At cafés, I would share my ideas on designing and making hats
Etienne would attend and both were enthusiastic in practical ways
Arthur invested in my designs and helped establish a business
In 1909, I opened my first millinery shop at Rue Cambon, Paris

Although I knew little about branding, I called it Chanel Modes
The hats that I created were worn by celebrated French actresses
In effect, they were my advertising models
Pictures of them wearing my hats appeared in magazines
Demand increased, and business grew
New shops were opened with much fanfare and success
It was an exciting time and the days flew by quickly
In 1913, I introduced women's sportswear into my Deauville shop
By the age of 30, I had a chain of shops, including one in Biarritz
It was a career that took me from poverty to riches
Then, the threat of poverty arose again
In 1914, the First World War commenced
It ruined my business
It also ruined France and the lives of those who fought to defend it
The fighting against the Germans was fierce and disastrous
Many were killed, both on the field of battle and in the streets
People needed help to treat their injuries
Along with other women, I volunteered to become a nurse
We tended soldiers with dreadful injuries
Also, we helped many civilians caught in the crossfire
Once the war was over, I tried to re-establish my business
New designs were developed
Jewellery, perfume and textiles were areas for expansion
The more relaxed clothing designs attracted younger women
In 1922, I introduced Chanel No 5 perfume, developed by Ernest Beaux
It became very popular and generated considerable income
Pierre Wertheimer became my partner in the jewellery business
However, as the years went by I was unhappy with the business contract
It was 1924 and people were becoming interested in my work
In 1925, I was invited to design stage costumes for Cocteau's *Antigone*
Other designs, like the Chanel cardigan, became popular
There were, of course, ups and downs, not least in my love life
I enjoyed the company of many handsome men
But, I could never settle down to marry any of them
Designing clothes and running the business was exciting
Innovating to help women look their best was my aim
Some of the changes in fashion raised both questions and eyebrows
Like replacing the corset with more easy-to-wear suits and dresses

In 1926, I introduced the 'little black dress', which became well known
It was described as sultry, seductive and sexy
Also, the cardigan, many said, stamped my signature on fashion
My job was to help women look beautiful and confident
Savoir vive
Savoir faire

However, further economic problems arose in 1929
The stock market crash reduced people's incomes
The business took time to recover during the 1930s
During this time, I travelled looking for new designs
My new ideas were displayed in Paris
As a result, the House of Chanel in Rue Cambon became well-known
It was further enhanced in 1932 by our jewellery exhibition
The number of staff continued to grow
More of my time was spent organising than designing

By 1935, I had over 4000 people working at Chanel
It had become a substantial business
My life was a merry-go-round of meetings and dinner parties
Just when we thought the business was secure, the Germans invaded
Yet again, France was brought to its knees
Businesses closed, families were torn apart and lives were wrecked
I felt it was time to retire
During the Second World War, I continued to live in Paris
It was a tough and difficult time
Many lived for the moment, not knowing what lay ahead
Others kept a low profile, but conspired against the Nazis
I was 57 and recognised the dangers
Hans von Dincklage, a German officer, became my lover
I was heavily criticised for that
To reduce the problems, I went to live in Switzerland
It did not stop me working on designs
In due course, I decided retirement was too boring
Therefore, in my 60s, I started again
The Coco Chanel brand name was established and became stronger
In 1954, when I was 71, my designs again were leading the way
The Chanel suit and the bell-bottomed pants became popular
More women were entering business and needed new fashions
Chanel became a name that stood for quality, elegance and identity
In 1957, we won a Fashion Oscar
As I had no family, my work was central to my existence
For 30 years, I lived at the Ritz Hotel, close to my Paris shop
Of course, it cost a fortune
But, one must live where one is secure and happy
Work was the interest that kept me alive
It gave me a purpose, as well as fame and fortune
In 1970, aged 87, I launched the No 19 perfume
Although time was running out for me, the organisation continued on
Reflecting the quality and hard work of everyone involved
It was an exciting life
One that enabled me to go from rags to riches
From poverty to plenty
From a convent smock to *haute couture*
From the poorhouse to high society.

Caroline Chisholm
1808–1874

I emigrated to Sydney, Australia in 1838
Sydney was founded as a convict colony
Great Britain had used it as a prison since 1788
It was still a rough and ready town when we arrived
It was 10,000 miles from England, where I was born
Each day, new ships with immigrants arrived
Some were free settlers like our family
But, many were convicts, held in chains
I made it my job to meet people at the quayside
Both the convicts and the free settlers
All needed help, particularly the young orphan girls
What could I offer?
A smile, a friendly word, some advice and practical help
I knew what it was like to be an immigrant
There were many problems everyone had to face
We had our two boys with us
Tragically my daughter had died while we were in India
To me, Sydney seemed like a mad house in paradise
The sun shone, but all around there was chaos
Convicts were marched under guard in one direction
Voluntary settlers were wandering around looking for help
People staggered off the boats, after months at sea
A number of people were ill and in need of assistance
Younger people had more energy and opportunity
I was 31 years of age at the time
It was so different from Northampton, my home town in England
My family were very religious
They took me to the Evangelical Church
There I learned about Christian principles
Helping others who were less fortunate was important to me
When I met Archibald Chisholm, I converted to Catholicism
He was a Captain in the British Army
At 35 years of age, he was more worldly wise than me
When I was 22, he asked me to marry him

Caroline Chisholm

I agreed on the condition that I could do philanthropic work
That is what I had in mind when we arrived in Sydney
Arriving on the SS *Emerald Isle* I knew it would not be easy
My husband had been working in Madras, India
So, I knew a lot about poverty and poor living conditions
By nature, I was an organizer
In Madras, I had set up a place of learning
The Female School of Industry for Daughters of Soldiers
It seemed that Sydney was sorely in need of such a school
Most of the young women arriving in the colony had little education
Neither did they have many skills to get a job
Most of the female convicts were thieves
The free settlers came with good intentions, but were ill prepared
After 50 years, Sydney was still a prison colony
Unless people knew you, they were suspicious
They wanted to know if you had a convict background
Indeed, having convict parents was a black mark
In effect, there were three sides of Sydney:
The settlers, the convicts and the aborigines
The latter were at the bottom of the social ladder
But there were other outcasts, particularly orphaned girls
What could be done to help?
In 1841, I proposed the Female Immigrant's Home
Governor Gipps and his wife gave their support
Despite opposition from others, we pressed ahead
I gained access to some old barracks
It provided shelter for 96 girls supported by public subscription
We ran the only free employment agency in Sydney
Gaining jobs for the girls was how I made space for newcomers
On my white horse, called Captain, I rode around asking for support
Visits to the bush enabled me to find places of work for my girls
Within a year, I was able to close the home for girls
As new people arrived, I was able to place them into work
Robert Towns gave me land to settle 23 families
However, an application to the Government for more land was rejected
During the 1840s, I was able to help about 14,000 people
More needed to be done
Political reform was required to improve conditions for immigrants

Therefore, in 1846, I set sail for London with my husband
Power over the Sydney colony resided 10,000 miles away
On our long voyage, I had time to reflect
Convict ships had ceased, and more free settlers were arriving
Therefore, it was important to assist them
They were the future of the great land 'downunder'
On arrival, I met with politicians
They arranged for me to meet influential people
In speeches to the House of Lord's Committee, I outlined the issues

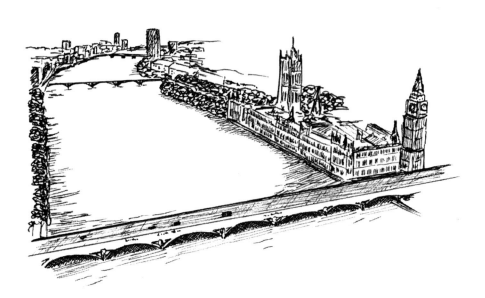

Some improvements were made to encourage family emigration
That was better than individuals roaming the streets of Sydney
Also, help needed to be given to young immigrants
Particularly young women, some of whom turned to prostitution
In 1849, the Family Colonisation Loan Society was established
Charles Dickens gave me his support and promoted its work
A ship owner, W. S. Lindsay, built the *Caroline Chisholm* sailing boat
Its maiden voyage in 1853 had many young girls on board

They came from the Jewish Ladies Benevolent Society
They sailed under the new laws of the Passenger Act of 1852
In England, some positive changes had been made
But, what was happening in Australia?
Indeed should I return to supervise the new developments?
It would have been easier for me to stay in Britain
By that time, I was the mother of five children
Therefore, I had my hands full in more senses than one
However, duty called and we set off on the long sea voyage
In 1854, I returned on the *Ballarat* ship bound for Melbourne
Over 900 pounds in subscriptions had been collected

I guarded it carefully
There were many people in need of finances
Over 3000 people had emigrated under the Loan Society
My husband was on the quay waiting to welcome me
He had returned in 1851 to work as a Colonial Agent
Archibald was delighted to see the family again
His news worried me
Gold fever had broken out and thousands of people had arrived
I was told that women and children needed help
Therefore, I set out on a tour of the goldfields

Many settlers lived in shacks or tents
Conditions in the mining areas were basic
Most people were living in makeshift tents
It was tough and rough living and particularly bad for the children
I proposed some shelter sheds
Elsewhere, I could see improvements
Life in Sydney was developing
However, women did not have the vote
They were treated as second class citizens
Medical facilities were few and far between
In the countryside, living conditions were still basic
But, an example had been set
The money I had raised was being used to help
However, I began to feel unwell
In 1857, a kidney disease was diagnosed
For a long period of time my energy levels were low
It was a difficult time, but I slowly improved
During that time, we ran a local shop to make a living
By July 1862, I felt strong enough to open a girl's school
It was very satisfying, once again, to be of help
After a few years, I knew it was time to move on
We decided to return to the UK
Arriving in 1866, we lived in Liverpool
It was a great contrast to the vast outback of Australia
But, the social problems were similar
The same was true in London where we lived next
Increasingly I needed help, as frailty set in
In the evenings, I reflected on my life
The days under the Indian sun
Then, our migration to Australia
Moving to the colonial town of Sydney
Caring for my family of four boys and two girls
Providing support for immigrants
Helping young girls in need
Persuading politicians in high places to help
Supported throughout by my husband
All the time, working to help others in need
It was all part of a rich life lived in modest circumstances.

Marie Curie
1867–1934

My mother died when I was nine years old
Tuberculosis, they said
I saw what it did to her
The continual coughing, the gradual decline
There was no cure, but it set me thinking
Could I make a contribution to save others?
My parents registered my name as Marya Salomee Sklodowska
I was their fifth child, of five, born at the Freta Boarding School
The apartment was part of my mother's salary, as the Principal
We lived in Warsaw, Poland, at that time occupied by the Russians
My mother, a musician, and father, a mathematician, were patriots
Despite this, we had to take in boarders to pay the bills
Father had lost his job as a teacher
Living in humble circumstances, we wanted our freedom
For me, it came by way of science
An unusual activity for a girl in those days
My cousin, Jozef Boguski, encouraged my interest in science
He was the Director of the Warsaw Museum and I did experiments there
However, in Poland, access to university education in science was limited
There were no places for females
There was an underground 'Floating University'
The name given to a network of people who taught each other
We moved from one house to another and shared our knowledge
To progress, it was necessary to go to another country
My sister, Bronia, had left to study in Paris
To assist her, I worked as a governess and sent her some money
First with a lawyer's family in Kraków, then for two years in Ciechanów
There, I fell in love with Kazimierz Zorawski, the son of a relative
We wanted to marry, but his family disapproved, as I was poor
So, I moved to Sopot, in the north of Poland
For a year, I was governess to the Fuchs family
Working by day, studying by night and living on the minimum
In the meantime, my sister married and invited me to Paris
At the age of 25, I went to live with her before renting a garret

Marie Curie

Eventually, I gained entrance to Sorbonne University
It was the start of my advanced studies in science
Studying during the day, tutoring in the evening
Qualifying in Mathematics during 1894
Later working at the Lippman Institute
Hard work in an unfamiliar country
Trying to understand in a foreign language
Living in poor conditions
Yet, determined to succeed
Crystallography and magnetism were my initial interests
I was also drawn by the magnetism of a quiet, rather shy, tutor
Pierre Curie was his name
He encouraged me to study the energy in iron ore
It meant trying to isolate radioactive substances
To do so required toiling over a giant vat of molten iron ore
Hard work in a shed or the open air
Little did I know that was a blessing
The substances in the vat gave off a poisonous gas
Through our interest in science, we talked about research
The more we talked, the more I liked Pierre
A chemistry of a different kind from that of our research
A union of hearts, not just heads
Before long, we were engaged and married in 1895
Pierre was 36 years of age and I was 28
It was also the start of a scientific partnership
Happiness, after years in the wilderness of lonely endeavour
Within a short time, I realised that I was pregnant
Our daughter, Irene, was born in 1897
That was the year I gained my Physics Doctorate
Head and heart, science and family, *tout ensemble*
We had the energy and ideas to pursue science into new areas
Working in what a colleague described as 'a stable or potato cellar'
The temperature in winter fell below zero
We searched for the frontier of radioactivity
Others were doing the same
In 1896, Becquerel accidentally discovered radioactivity
Our studies built on this through interesting applications
'Pitchblende' does not sound too exciting

But, working with it, I saw the future
Radium and polonium were detected in 1898
The latter was named by me after Poland
Magic material, but what could we do with it?
More experiments showed it was powerful on human skin problems
Radium was used to burn off cancers
'Curie therapy' was the popular name given to the treatment
Work with Dabierge, another colleague, and my husband, continued

Pure radium was discovered
I was awarded the Nobel Prize in 1903
It was shared with Pierre and Becquerel, for their contributions
We used the money to support more research and needy students
Radioactivity was not a chemical, but the property of an atom
Nature's gift, if only we could harness it
At home, there were problems, as I had a miscarriage in 1903
Fortunately, after recovery, our daughter Eve was born in 1904
It looked as if we could combine family and professional life

But disaster struck in 1906
Pierre was killed by a horse, in a freak accident
As a single mother of two children, I was distraught
Sorbonne University offered me Pierre's position
The first female Professor, I continued his work
But, the French Science Academy ignored my work
Sexism and being Polish, I think, outweighed scientific discoveries
But maybe also because there was gossip
For a long time after Pierre's death, I was in shock
As a single mother, I tried to balance work and family life
It was not easy
Through my work, I got to know Paul Langevin, a fellow scientist
He had been a student of Pierre's
In my dark days, his support helped me though
Paul was five years younger than me
Gradually our relationship became more than platonic
In 1910, he left his wife and we had a relationship
People in the science community knew
The gossip developed into a so-called scandal
Hard to believe in Paris, where an affair was *de rigueur*
Personal and professional issues became confused
But not so for the second Nobel Prize, which I was awarded in 1911
This time for chemistry, measuring the atomic weight of radium
My work on radioactivity and x-rays continued
During the First World War, it was used to assess serious injuries
With my daughter Irene, I set up X-ray vans
We trained 150 radiographers
Dreadful days, seeing the effects of the bombing and shooting
Trying to save our valiant soldiers against the German invaders
After the war, recognition for my work came from the USA
As well as travel to many countries to encourage scientists
That became very important
Therefore my discoveries were not patented for self-gain
We needed as many people as possible to help
Advancing the boundaries to cure illness with radiotherapy treatments
Reducing pain and suffering, extending people's lives and other uses
Reflected in The Radium Institute,
The organisation that I helped establish in Paris during 1914

Another was established in Warsaw in 1932
My sister Bronia became its founding director
In addition, my daughter Irene became a scientist
She won the Nobel Prize for artificial radioactivity in 1935
Marking an achievement of which Pierre would be proud
A mark of progress for which so many gave their lives
Working with radioactive dangerous materials
Developing the forces of nature to help improve people's lives
En route, I was a mother, scientist, teacher and technical specialist
I also worked in managerial roles and as a representative
All part of a life that opened up new avenues for all.

Emilie du Chatelet
1706–1749

A woman should not compete with a man
Her education should fit her for being a wife
A woman should have children and look after her husband
Those were the views and attitudes that surrounded me
Education for a girl was seen of little benefit
I was therefore fortunate that my father gave me opportunities
Being born in Paris to a noble family helped
Father was Principal Secretary to King Louis XIV
He, and my mother, gave me a long name
Gabrielle-Emilie Le Tonnelier de Breteuil
My parents soon realised that I was gifted with figures
Likewise, I mastered Latin, English, Spanish and Italian
Greek and German were other languages I understood
I did not need much sleep, and learnt quickly
Dancing was a hobby, and I also played the harpsichord
Singing opera and roles as an amateur actress were fun
Mathematics though was my main interest
Solving mathematical puzzles was fascinating
Sometimes my knowledge was used to gamble
Equally, I enjoyed flirting with young men
It was a pleasure to receive attention
Likewise, the men showed that they enjoyed my attentions
There were many opportunities at the Versailles Court
By the age of 19, however, I was married
It was arranged by my family
My husband, the Marquis du Chastellet, was 34
He was an army officer and owned a number of estates
Within two years, I was a mother
Our son was followed by the birth of our daughter
When I was 27, I had another son
In that sense, I was fulfilling the normal expectations
That was not sufficient for me
My husband and I had little in common
He was often away, and it was lonely staying at home

Emilie du Chatelet

The action, for the aristocracy, was at Court
Politics was far more exciting than domestic work
Traditionally, it was a man's game, but I decided to join in
To discuss politics with the men, I had to dress as a man
Only then was I allowed entry to their coffee houses
Of course, there were many flirtatious opportunities
Extra marital liaisons added spice to my life
At the age of 24, I had an affair with the Duc de Richelieu
It lasted for over a year
That was the third one since I had married
My husband was no doubt having his affairs also
I believed in equality
Our marriage was increasingly one of convenience
In between, I was determined to continue with mathematics
The most knowledgeable tutors were engaged to help me
Pierre Louis de Maupertuis was a renowned astronomer
He found me a challenging pupil
That was my nature
Samuel Koenig, another tutor, was upset with my challenges
It resulted in our parting company
However, one eminent person made me welcome
Voltaire, the great writer, enjoyed my company
We met in 1733, when I was 28 and he was 39
Officially, he called me Madame du Chatelet
In reality, it was far more personal
I became his mistress
Initially, we enjoyed socialising in Paris
But our affair shocked many, and gossip surrounded us
Voltaire was also in danger of arrest for his writings
It was important that we had time alone
I invited him to live at my country chateau
We went to Cirey sur Blaise, far from Paris
It was a meeting of minds, as well as hearts
Philosophy, religion and ethics were key topics
In 1737, I wrote a research paper
Dissertation sur la nature et la propagation du feu
My study of fire led to predictions about infra-red radiation
I could concentrate for hours on such work

My young family were growing up
They began to understand the relationship with Voltaire
His real name was Francois-Marie Arouet
We both became famous under our pen names
With Voltaire, I wrote a book about Newton's work

Published in 1738, it was called *Elements of Newton's Philosophy*
Two years later, I wrote another book to help my son
He was 13 years old, and interested in science
The book, *Institutions de Physique*, covered lessons in physics
A new law of energy was proposed

This challenged the age old principles of Newton
Most of my writing was done in the day
Many hours were spent studying the work of Leibniz and Newton
A major task was to translate one of Newton's books into French
It was called *The Principia*

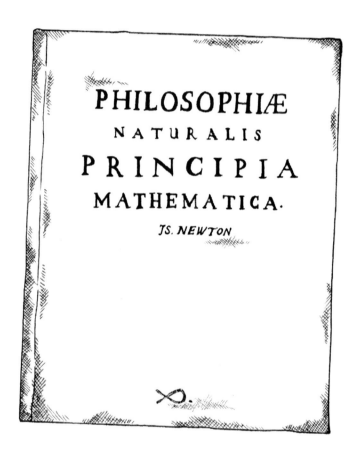

It dealt with geometry, calculus, optics and orbital mechanics
Translation from the Latin version was demanding
In addition, I added an 'Algebraical Commentary'
Physics was also a subject of great interest
It was not all hard work, as we entertained many guests

One of these was Marquis de Saint-Lambert
He was a courtier and poet
In 1748, I realised that I was very attracted to him
He became my lover, and I became pregnant
Voltaire was understanding and supportive
My concern was that my husband would be angry
To avoid this, I convinced him that the child was his
He seemed to believe me, but maybe he had his doubts
After all, we had spent little time together
In September 1749, aged 43, I gave birth to a daughter
It seemed that everything was normal
However, I took ill with an embolism
My daughter also became ill and died
So much left unsaid and uncompleted
A life searching for truth and love
A life of highs and lows
But, never slow or dull.

Sally Hemings
1772–1835

The Master had sent a note
The overseer of slaves read it to me
'Please arrange for my daughter Mary to be escorted, to Paris'
I looked at him wondering what it had to do with me
'You have been chosen to take Mary,' he added
I did not know what to say
I just asked, 'Where is Paris?'
'It is the capital of France,' said the overseer
As a slave, I had no choice but to obey
I was told it would be a long journey
'You will be on a boat for about six weeks,' the overseer told me
'We must be going to the end of the Earth,' I replied
My mother was surprised and upset when I told her
'It is a great responsibility that the Master has given you,' she said
'Look after Mary well, for she is your niece'
We started to pack some clothes
'You know that your brother, James, is working for the Master'
'Please give him my love,' she said with a tear in her eye
To me, the journey seemed like a great adventure
I had never been outside of the British colony of Virginia
All of my young life had been lived on plantations
Born to a slave, I accepted that was my fate like so many others
But, would leaving the plantation change anything in my life?
In the next few months, I was to find it did in amazing ways
Firstly, the Master had arranged for me to have new clothes
Also, I was given money to pay the bills on our journey
As a slave girl, I had never had money to spend
On the day of departure, Mary and I were farewelled in great style
The overseer and the slaves cheered and waved us on our way
We were taken to the port in a horse and buggy
The ship, with its sails blowing in the wind, looked elegant
Once we were in the middle of the Atlantic Ocean, I felt ill
The waves were huge and I thought we would drown
The ship soared upwards and then plunged rapidly downwards

Sally Hemings

When it was calmer, I walked around the deck
What would I do in France?
Would they have slaves?
Would the people understand me when I spoke to them?
Apart from walking and talking with Mary, there was little to do
Our ship docked first in England, where friends of the Master met us
Mary and I were amazed at the city and the large number of people
Adrien Petit, the Master's Butler, was there to meet us
He escorted us from London to Paris
A journey to another new world
Both Mary and I were again surprised by what we saw
So many people, all rushing, as if in a race
So many large buildings crushed together
All around, there was a foul smell
Then, I saw people tipping their waste into the narrow streets
That created mud heaps of dirt and stench
It was all so different from the clean countryside in Virginia
Although the daughter of a slave, I lived on a grand estate
My mother, Betsy, said my father was a white man, John Wayles
He owned land at Guinea Plantation, Cumberland, Virginia
Of course, my mother, a slave, was not married to my father
He had been married three times before
When his third wife died, he approached my mother in 1762
As one of his slaves, she became his concubine
It was, however, a long and productive relationship
During a period of more than ten years, they had six children
Three boys and three girls, of which I was the last
Prior to that, with his first wife, John Wayles had a daughter
Born in 1748, she was called Martha
In 1766, she married, but her husband died five years later
She inherited his estate and, in 1773, part of her father's
That included the slaves, including my mother and me
She married again and her husband became our new Master
We went with her to Virginia, as slave servants in 1776
That was quite normal at the time
Mother worked on the Master's 5,000 acre estate
So did my brothers and sisters
We were all related to Martha, as we had the same father

Therefore, I was a half-sister to the Master's wife
Martha had six children, including a daughter, called Mary
Sadly, in 1782, Martha died
Being very upset, the Master left the Virginia plantation
It was said that he went to Washington and then to work overseas
Years passed without him returning to the Monticello Estate
Then, out of the blue, came a message

It was a surprise to hear I had been chosen to take his daughter to Paris
After all, I was a slave just approaching 15 years of age
When told that I had to go to Paris, it was a shock
I did not know what to say
However, it was not for me to question the Master's wishes
I talked to Mary, his daughter, who was eight years of age

'Your father wants me to escort you to France,' I said
Therefore, in 1787, with some anxiety, we set off from rural Virginia
People were surprised to see two young girls on a voyage
Particularly, sailing through the stormy waters of the Atlantic Ocean
We were pleased to reach dry land and be escorted to Paris
On arrival in pleasant July weather, the Master came out to meet us
Mary was delighted to see him and he held her high
Also, his older daughter, Patsy, was with him
She had accompanied him to Paris two years earlier
It was a happy family reunion
The Master then looked at me
'Thank you for bringing Mary to be with me,' he said
It was the first time he had ever spoken to me personally
At home, he would not talk publicly to the child of a slave
We rode to Paris in a horse-drawn coach
Mary and I waved to people in the streets
'Why are we here?' Mary asked her father
'It is my job to represent our country in France,' he replied
'Yes,' said Patsy, 'Father has an important job'
The coach arrived at a stylish residence on the Champs-Élysées
My new home, in a fine apartment, was well furnished
There, I met my brother James and he took my hand warmly
'I am working here as the Master's chef,' he said
I passed on mother's message and he told me of life in Paris
Afterwards, the Master sent for me
'Please look after Mary and help her,' he said
'I will arrange for you to be taught needlework and cooking'
'They will be important skills for the work you will do,' he advised
One of the servants told me that, in France, I was a 'Ladies Maid'
Indeed, to my surprise, I was paid a small wage
For the first time, I had my own money and my own room
To really help Mary, I needed to become educated
But, would the Master allow it?
Slaves in Virginia were not taught how to read or write
Education was not seen as important, even for white girls
In Paris, those things did not apply
Indeed, Patsy attended a convent boarding school
Mary also went to the school for a while

So, we did not see much of them during the week days
Each day I was trained by the other staff members
Some spoke English and they helped me learn basic French
They asked me what it was like to be a slave in America
One of them said that, in France, I was a free person under their law
Indeed, I could go anywhere, with the Master's permission

Most days, I went to do the shopping with a colleague
Although a slave in name, I soon learned that my role was different
The only difference was that people knew I was from abroad
My darker skin led many people to make comments
Gradually, I began to understand what they were saying

Within a few months, I could converse a little in French
Mary returned and had some lessons at the residence
By listening to Mary's tutors, I also learnt to read and write
Ironically, I could write better in French than in English
Also, I made friends with people in Paris of my own age
They helped me learn many new things about life
One thing was obvious
The poor hated the rich
Just like the slaves hated the landowners at home
But, for me, Paris was a place where I felt free
During vacations, Mary had lessons at home and I escorted her
After a while, she asked to have all her lessons at home
In that way, I learnt about mathematics and geography
One of the tutors helped us chart the voyage that we had made
The map also showed other countries, including those in Africa
The tutor explained how slaves were captured there and transported
For the first time, I understood how slavery started
However, in France, I felt a new person
Much more confident and knowledgeable
Yet, I was still a black slave girl from Virginia
Still under the rule of my Master
He seemed a very busy man, but treated me kindly
Each day, he had many meetings
Officials from the French Government often arrived to see him
He also visited their offices, dressed in fine clothes
There were also grand ceremonial occasions
Also, the Master hosted dinner parties for dignitaries at his residence
One day, the Master called me to his office
He said, 'On Saturday, I have tickets for the theatre'
'The French Government has asked me to attend'
'I would like you to accompany me'
The invitation came as a great surprise
The Master was 30 years older than me
He was a man of the world and I was a slave girl
I hesitated, not sure what to say
Then, I realised this was Paris
I was not a slave in France
'Thank you,' I said, 'I look forward to it'

'Good,' he replied, 'I will make the arrangements'
The next day, a lady arrived and asked to see me
She said that I was to have a new dress and measured me
The Master also arranged for me to have special jewellery
Within a few days, a beautiful dress arrived
Mary was excited and helped me prepare for the evening
A grand coach and horses took us to the theatre
On arrival, the Master held out his hand to help me descend
'This is my niece from America,' he said to a dignitary
The Frenchmen replied, '*Vous avez une jolie fille*'
A pretty girl, indeed, was how I felt
I noticed that the Master had not introduced me as a 'ladies maid'
Nor had he mentioned that I was one of his slaves
It was like a fairy tale and I smiled to all around
Could this be really happening to me?
For the first time, I was in a theatre watching a play
On the return journey, the Master asked if I had enjoyed it
'Yes,' I said, 'But, it was difficult to understand the play'
'My understanding of French needs to improve,' I added
'I will arrange for you to have some lessons,' said the Master
The visit to the theatre was the first of many such events
The next time, he invited me to an opera
Yet another beautiful dress and more jewellery arrived
At the opera, there were more dignitaries and more compliments
Having had some French lessons, I joined in the conversation
I was being treated as a lady, not as a ladies maid or a slave
During the interval, other ladies talked to me
Some invited me to meet them for what they called '*une reunion*'
Sometimes, we met in cafes, sometimes at their homes
They asked me about my life in America
'I live on a grand estate,' I said
However, I did not mention that I was a slave
Having learned about diplomacy, I did not go into personal details
At further meetings, the ladies told me about their lives
Most were married, but said that they did not love their husbands
Their marriages had been arranged, for family and political reasons
Indeed, the ladies were quite open about their relationships
Most of them had lovers and, in some cases, more than one

They said that their husbands also had '*les affaires d'amours*'
Of course, from time to time, children came along
Who was the father?
The husband or the lover?
It was better not to ask and so that was the way it was
At first, I was shocked, but came to realise the reality
I was in France
It was the French way of dealing with issues
Indeed, was it so different than relationships at home in Virginia?
The slave owners had both wives and slave mistresses
Of course, children were born
Few questions were asked about who their fathers were
It was all part of the accepted way of life
Marriages and mistresses, side by side
I wondered if it would ever happen to me
If so, it seemed a long way away
Or was it?
One winter evening, the Master called me to his office
'There is a Grand Court Ball in about two months,' he said
'I would like you to accompany me'
'Thank you, but I do not know how to dance,' I replied
'Arrangements can be made for you to have lessons,' he said
Within a few days, a dance tutor arrived
Music filled the apartment everyday and I gained confidence
Also, the dressmaker arrived again
Another beautiful dress was made
Servants brought it in and helped me to put it on
I swirled round the room dancing
Looking in the mirror, I could hardly believe it
It was everything that a teenage girl could ask for
On the evening, we went to the Grand Court Ball in a coach
The Master took my hand and led me inside
The orchestra was playing waltz music
Everyone was extremely well dressed
I wondered if the guests would notice that I was a slave
The Master did not treat me as one
Instead, he invited me on to the dance floor
All the lessons and practice were put to the test

He smiled, as we waltzed around
Afterwards, he talked with the hosts
'This is my niece, Sally,' he told them
'She is here as a companion for my daughter'
At home, I was always regarded as a slave
Unlike many slaves, I was well-treated and never beaten
Now in Paris, I was a niece, a companion and a ladies maid
I had to pinch myself to make sure that I was not dreaming
On the way home, the Master talked about the evening
'Sally, you danced very well tonight'
It was the first time he had complimented me
'Thank you for inviting me and for the beautiful dress,' I said
After the success of the first Ball, there were other invitations
Each time the Master arranged for me to have a new dress
Within a short time, I realised that I had another role
Outside the leaves were falling off the trees, as Autumn had arrived
Late one day, the Master asked me to visit him in his office
'Sally, the King of France has sent me an invitation,' he said
'It is an important event and I would like you to accompany me'
'That sounds exciting,' I replied, now more at ease with him
'Where will we be going?' I enquired
'The Royal Palace at Versailles, outside of Paris,'
'What dress should I take?' I asked
'You will need a formal gown,' he replied
'I will arrange for the dressmaker to create one for you'
As I was about to leave, he said, 'One other thing'
'The King has asked that we be his guests for the weekend'
'Please pack whatever you will need for two or three days away'
I raced off to prepare and made a list
Shoes, jewellery, dresses and, of course, my night clothes
Before the event, the Master arranged a special tutor
A well-dressed lady came to see me
'I have been asked to teach you Court etiquette,' she said
I was taught many things, such as how to converse with the King
It was a good job that I had already taken French lessons
Once again, I was well prepared and set off in the Master's coach
On arrival, I was amazed by the size and grandeur of the Palace
The servants showed us to our living area

It was magnificent, with paintings and beautiful furniture
But, I soon realised one important thing
There were no separate bedrooms
It was assumed the guests would have their wives or mistresses
So, that night, I guessed that I might have another role
A role that my mother had mentioned when discussing our family
She was a slave mistress to Mr. Wayles and had his children
For her, there was little choice
But, in France, I had a choice
I was approaching 17 years of age
Fully developed physically and catching the eyes of Frenchmen
Under their law, I was free to choose my friends
So was my Master able to choose, as his wife had died
Although he was kind, I was not his fiancée
Neither of us had illusions about marriage
Nevertheless, we enjoyed each other's company
No doubt, I made him feel young again
For his part, he helped transform me from a girl to a woman

Indeed, not just in the bedroom, but also in society
The theatre, the opera, the grand balls and dances
Beautiful dresses and diamonds glittering in the candlelight
Plus, new hair styles and perfume
At last, I knew what my French lady friends meant
It was not necessary to be married to enjoy the benefits
Why should I object?
In the mean streets of Paris, there were poor girls starving
At home, young slave girls were growing old in the fields
Life for me, as the French said, was 'belle et tres agreable'
I felt a new woman in a new land
There were more social events
On each occasion, the Master took me as his guest
No longer a ladies maid or just his niece

He introduced me as a friend of the family
Of course, the French knew exactly what that meant
They had many ways of describing such relationships
Courtesan, concubine, mistress
A special woman in the life of an important man
Only I knew that he was my slave Master
Invitations to parties and balls became regular events
Visits to '*les chateaux*' and the nobility in the countryside
The French people wanted to know about our country
At the dinner table, the Master told them about the changes
'America is now independent,' he told them
'The war against the British has been won'
Everyone would raise their glasses to the birth of our new country
I wondered whether 'independence' would change my life
My mother was still a slave and so were thousands of others
Africans were still being captured and transported to America
If I returned, would I still be a slave?
Of course, I kept such concerns to myself
After dinner, the talk was more about the situation in France
There was great unrest in the villages, towns and cities
The people in high society feared a civil war
The gap between the rich and poor was immense
Just like the gap between the landowners and slaves in Virginia
Before midnight, my Master would thank his hosts
Taking my arm, we would retire to our shared room
Less timid than on the first occasion, I knew what to expect
He was always kind and considerate, respecting my needs
There was a time and a place for the formal and the personal
Never rushed, he helped me develop emotionally and physically
Indeed, I found the visits and the evenings most enjoyable
Experiencing what it was like to be a society woman
Since arriving in France, I had moved up the social ladder
From slave to ladies maid and from a niece to a companion
But, I had also gained a privileged position
I had become the Master's chosen woman, a courtesan
He had taken me to the theatre, to the opera and the Grand Balls
More than that, I had met the King of France and stayed at his palace
The Master had made me a woman of standing in all respects

What more could a slave girl ask for?
Or, was it all an illusion?
In France, the poor people were angry
It was 1789 and on July 14th the Bastille prison in Paris was stormed
The crowd went berserk and aristocrats were guillotined
The French Revolution had begun

Liberté, Egalité, Fraternité, chanted the mob
Each day, more people were killed as the terror continued
One night, in bed, the Master whispered in my ear
'We must leave for home before the violence gets worse'

Within a month, we had packed
On September 28th we set sail from Le Havre across the Atlantic Ocean
It was a long and rough sea voyage on board the *SS Clermont*
During the two months, there was time to consider
What would happen when we arrived in Norfolk, Virginia?
Would the Master still want me?
There was good cause to be concerned
I was pregnant
Before leaving the ship, on November 23rd, I told him
He nodded, but did not say anything
Soon as we were on land, many people rushed to meet him
I heard one person say to him
'George Washington will be inaugurated as our first President'
He came over to talk to Mary, Patsy and myself
The Master told us that he was required in the capital
'The President has appointed me as Secretary of State,' he said
Before leaving, he gave Patsy a letter and then waved goodbye
We started on the long journey back to the plantation in Virginia
On arrival, the Master's daughters received a great reception
I returned to the slave's quarters
Nothing seemed to have changed
The world was still black and white
Black people were still slaves working in the fields
White people were in charge of the estate
There was no *Liberté*, *Egalité*, or *Fraternité* and I was still a slave
However, I had learned many things
I could read, write and do mathematics
In addition, I could speak French
Also, I knew a lot about the theatre, opera and dancing
Not to mention my roles as companion, niece and courtesan
What should I do with these skills?
I decided it was best to keep it all secret
People would only talk if they knew
It would create problems for me and the Master
Slaves were not allowed to be educated in Virginia
Mother was delighted to see me again
She smiled when I told her I was pregnant
That was of more interest than my experiences in Paris

She seemed to understand how it had happened and never asked
The Master's letter was given to his officials by Patsy
Instructions that indicated I was to work at the big house
My mother and I were given domestic duties
From time to time, the Master would visit
During the day time, he was always busy and we never spoke
At night time, when others were asleep, he came to see me
He had allocated me a room of my own
Secluded from the rest of the mansion, it was private
We talked of our time in France
Occasionally, he would tell me what was happening in the capital
Never did he mention any plans to abolish slavery
Therefore, my child was born a slave
Within a short period, she took ill and died
I felt responsible, albeit there was nothing that could be done
The Master visited and prayed with me as I cried
Was that to be the end of our affair?
He was now a powerful leader in our new nation
No doubt, he was attractive to many women in the capital
Before he left to go north, he came to see me again
'As you know, attitudes in Virginia are hard to change'
'The landowners will not abolish slavery,' he said
'Also, marriage for slaves is not allowed in this State'
'But, I could arrange a relationship with another slave?'
He must have seen the look of horror on my face
Having tasted freedom in France, I knew what that meant
The ladies of Paris had told me all about arranged relationships
I shook my head
'I understand and value our time together,' he said
'But, if you wish, you can meet who you want on the plantation'
Again, I shook my head
'Indeed, if you want, I could give you and your mother freedom'
'Where would we go?' I asked
'How would we earn a living?'
This time, he shook his head
Taking me in his arms, he promised to look after me and my mother
Outside, there was a full moon
He left just as the sun began to rise

The first of many such meetings when he was not in the capital
Our next child was born in 1795
She was soon running round the estate
In the next 13 years, we had four more children
We named them Harriet, Beverly, Madison, Eston and Thomas
All our children were born between 1795 and 1808
Maybe some people guessed who their father was
After all, it was a small community
We were relatively isolated
Indeed, what we did was our business
One night in bed, the Master said: 'I will have to go away'
'Why is that?' I asked
'They want me to be the next President,' he replied
'Is that what you want?' I enquired
'If it will help the country, then I will do it,' he said
In 1805, he was elected President of the United States of America
As mother of the President's children, it was a proud day for me
However, I was not there to join in the celebrations
Nor was I seen at any public event
It would have ruined his reputation if I had visited the capital
Can you imagine what people would have said?
The President accompanied by a slave girl!
The President surrounded by his slave children!
Some insinuations were made
James T Callendar wrote an article
It was published in the *Washington Federalist* newspaper
However, he had no proof
We did not want newspaper headlines such as
'Slave Mother of President's Children'
Or, 'President Has Children with Unmarried Mother'
Therefore, I stayed on the plantation
The only city that I visited was Paris
It changed my life in some ways, but not in others
It was an interlude between slavery
It was the start of an incredible relationship
A relationship with a man who I trusted
One that continued for nearly 40 years
Indeed, it lasted longer than most marriages

A relationship with the most powerful man in the country
Except, he could not abolish slavery
If he had freed me, I would have had to leave Virginia
Because of his debts, he needed slaves to run his plantation
In all, he had over 100 slaves
However, he did what he could for our family
With his help, our daughters, Harriet and Beverley, escaped
Our sons stayed on the plantation
They were freed in the Master's Will
He died on July 4th 1826, aged 83

I was 53 years old and officially remained a slave
My best years were behind me
What would happen to me?
After the funeral, Patsy, the Master's daughter came to see me
She was the only person who really knew my secret
Her sister, Mary, had died in 1804, aged 26
Patsy had been in France, albeit at a convent school
She understood the relationship between me and her father
Particularly when we returned to the plantation

Especially, when I became pregnant
Occasionally, she would say something in French
We shared a special bond between us
A secret way of communicating important things
However, we never talked about my relationship
That was only a matter for me and the Master
At our meeting, Patsy had tears in her eyes
'My father asked me to give you your time,' she said
She handed me a letter written by the Master
It was a form of retirement for slaves
The letter allowed me to continue living in Virginia
So, it was that I moved to a house in Charlottesville
Once again, the Master had made the arrangements
I had plenty of time to reflect and remember
My life as a slave on a plantation and as a lady in Paris
Learning how to speak French, plus read and write
A sparkling time, meeting royalty and the nobility
Returning to Virginia to be a slave mother
The mother of the President's children
An amazing life with an amazing man.

Postscript
Sally Hemings died, without marrying, at 62 years of age in 1835.

Susannah Holmes
1764–1825

I was sent to a mixed-sex prison, in 1783
There were more men than women in the jail
One needed to be strong to survive
Henry Cable befriended me
We both came from a Suffolk village, called Surlingham
Before long, we were lovers
Not that there was much privacy in the jail
Henry had been in a gang of thieves, led by his father
The others were hung, but Henry, the youngest, was spared
We were both sent to Norwich Prison
I had also been sentenced to death for stealing
Because I was young, the judge recommended a reprieve
But, I still had to serve a long sentence
The prison was an overcrowded, filthy place
Despite the conditions, I gave birth to a son in February 1786
We named him Henry, after his father
Keeping him alive in prison was difficult
In mid 1786, we were told that we would be moved
'Where to?' I asked Mr Simpson, one of the jail officers
'You are going to New South Wales,' he replied
'Never heard of it,' I said
'It is at the other end of the Earth,' he added in a grim tone
In the next few days rumours began to circulate
We were being deported to a desolate island across the oceans
A life sentence by another name
In October, I was sent to Plymouth for deportation
It was a long 200 mile journey in a horse drawn truck
We bounced up and down on the cobbled roads
I tried to protect my son from the rain and wind
Mr John Simpson escorted us and did his best to help
However, when I arrived at the port there was a big shock
The Captain refused to let me take my son on board
He said that his list only referred to convicts
'The young boy has not committed any crimes,' he said with a snarl

Susannah Holmes

He ordered that my baby be taken from me
I screamed and cried, as I knew I would never see my child again
John Simpson, the prison officer, pleaded with the Captain
It was to no avail
Amazingly, Mr Simpson offered to help me
'Give me the baby,' he said, 'I will go to London and get permission'
I gave him my baby and he set off on the long 250 miles journey
Travelling by horse, it took him nearly two weeks
Arriving in London, he made enquiries on what to do
He discovered that Lord Sydney was in charge of deportations
Despite his best efforts, a formal meeting could not be arranged
Time was ticking by and John Simpson had little money
However, he would not be put off and decided on a bold approach
He went to his Lord Sydney's house and waited for him to appear
It was not an easy task for a local jailor to talk to a powerful man
When his Lordship saw John Simpson with my baby, he stopped
On hearing the problem, Lord Sydney agreed to let my son go with me
A deportation document was signed to be given to the ship's captain
In addition, he agreed the father of my son, Henry, should join me
Mr Simpson made the long return journey, resting at pubs *en route*
People heard his story and donated money and presents for my son
On December 25th 1786, Mr Simpson arrived with the permit
Amongst great joy and tears of relief, he gave me back my baby
It was the best Christmas present that I could ever receive
Mrs Jackson, who he met *en route*, was particularly helpful
She gave him a number of gifts
They included some money, valued at twenty pounds
Captain Sinclair said he would guard all the gifts during the journey
On Sunday 13th May 1787, a gun was fired and we set sail
For the next nine months, we rolled and tossed on the high seas
Dreadful damp days of sea sickness and despair
The waves crashed down on us and I feared for our lives
En route, we stopped at Tenerife in June 1787
Eight weeks later, we arrived in Rio de Janeiro
As prisoners, we were not allowed to leave the ship
Then, it was another long voyage to the Cape of Good Hope
There was nothing good about it and very little hope
Once again, we set sail across rough seas

For eight weeks, we did not see any land
The journey was a punishment in itself
Eventually, on January 18th 1788 we arrived at another prison
Botany Bay was 10,000 miles from England
All on the suggestion from Captain Cook and Joseph Banks

AUSTRALIA.

NEW SOUTH WALES
COLONY 1788

They had only spent a couple of days there in 1770
It was like arriving at another planet
Governor Phillip did not like the place and set off on a search
As a result, we moved to Port Jackson, which became known as Sydney
There were 12 ships and the men disembarked

But, the 191 women were kept on board for another week
On reaching shore, I quickly found my boyfriend Henry Cable
He was overjoyed to see me and our son
That night, he asked me to marry him
Happiness amongst so much desolation and danger
Governor Phillip agreed to our marriage
In Norwich Prison, it would not have been allowed
On February 10th 1788, both aged 19, we married
It was a Sunday and Reverend Richard Johnson officiated
Three other couples were also married
The first marriages in the colony, not yet a country
But, we had no home and there was no honeymoon
Violent storms with thunder and lightning were scary
There was little food and there were only a few tents to live in
It was no place to tend a baby and sanitation was non-existent
The first of many challenges and another one arose
The ship's Captain refused to give me the gifts and money
He denied all knowledge of receiving them
So began a key legal case in the history of Australia
Could a convicted prisoner sue a ship's captain?
Henry petitioned Governor Phillip to put the Captain on trial
To his credit, he did so on July 5th 1788
Would a convict's word be believed against that of a ship's captain?
The Court was an army officer, the church minister and an official
Captain Sinclair was found guilty and told to repay the money
I received 15 pounds of the original sum
However, it was incredible that we were able to gain justice
In England, the convict was legally dead, with no rights to sue
Despite the Captain being declared guilty, he was not made a convict
We had been jailed and sent 'down under' for far less
Others, including Henry's relatives, had been hung for similar crimes
Nevertheless, it was a momentous decision
Governor Phillip had set the mark for justice in the new colony
It showed the rule of law would prevail
It was the start of the principle of what we called a 'fair go'
Setting the standards, regardless of each person's position or rank
Yet, we were not equal in our new land
We were still convicts and there was no place to spend the money

The guards, the military and officials had great power over us
Each day was hard labour, usually in hot conditions
However, we wanted to increase our family
On December 5th 1788 our daughter Dianna was born
Times were tough as food was scarce
Our chances of surviving in the harsh conditions were low
The British Government had abandoned us
Governor Phillip, to his credit, did his best to manage the situation
However, because of the poor land, it was difficult to grow food
There were also dangers from attacks by the aboriginals
After two years, we were reduced to half rations
Only then did ships arrive with new convicts, but little food
We were creating a new society in a wilderness
Fortunately, some aborigines helped us learn some survival skills
The rest was up to our native wit and ability to learn quickly
But, we were still prisoners
The prison warders could be brutal and gave severe beatings
We were in the largest open-air prison in the world
On an island from which there was no escape
A place where illness could rarely be cured
It was best to accept the primitive conditions and work hard
Henry and I set up home and built our family
In 1791 our son Enoch was born
Tragically, he died when only two years old
However, my other children all survived infancy
In total, I had eight boys and three girls with the last born in 1806
By that time, I was 40 years of age
As a family, we formed a good team
I became emancipated after serving my sentence
As the mother of our 11 children, I led a full life
Henry served his 14 years and became a free man
He established a number of businesses and made a good living
We also lived at The Rampant Horse Hotel as licensees
He was appointed a constable
Later, we owned a farm, a trading business and a shop
We were a founding family of Australia and proud of it
With the money Mr Simpson had collected, we started a business
Gradually, improvements were made

Yet, there was still punishment and cruelty all around
We focused on our family
We were both determined to give our children a better life
I did not choose to be a 'Founding Mother' of Australia
But, I am proud to have done so
My thoughts, however, returned to England
I never saw my family, or the country of my birth, again
Mr Simpson, the prison warder was my hero
Sadly, he never knew what he really achieved
Like Henry and myself, I believe that he was a founder of Australia
If ever there was a true godfather it was John Simpson
He saved my son and helped form a new family in a new country.

Madame Lavoisier
1758–1836

At 13 years of age, I received a proposal of marriage
Count d'Amerval was a rich and powerful man
He was almost 40, nearly three times my age
My mother was not there to advise me, as she had died
At the age of three, I had been sent to a convent
My name tag read, Marie-Anne Pierette Paulze
After that, I was brought up under the guidance of the nuns
For ten years, I lived a religious and sheltered life
Therefore, the marriage proposal worried me
My father, a lawyer and financier, visited me from time to time
When he heard of the marriage proposal, he rejected the idea
His objections were met by threats from the Count
He said that my father could lose his Government job
A quick plan was devised to thwart the Count
It still involved marriage, but to another man
My father asked one of his colleagues if he would marry me
His name was Antoine Lavoisier
Aged 28, he was a nobleman with an interest in science
We met and he seemed kind and considerate
Our marriage took place on December 16th 1771
It was, at the time, more a matter of convenience than love
In 1775, my husband was appointed to a new and important job
Commissioner of the Royal Gunpowder and Saltpeter Administration
We went to live at the Arsenal in Paris
A significant move, given the revolutionary fervour of the time
I was 17 and beginning to understand the world outside the convent
Learning quickly about sexual matters and political issues
Most of all, realising that our marriage was more than a convenience
The more we were together, the more we fell in love
Each day, I learnt about my husband's work
Originally trained as a lawyer, he had turned to study science
As a chemist, he had established a laboratory
Observing his research work, I recorded the experiments
This helped to establish patterns and effects

Madame Lavoisier

His colleagues, *Messieurs* Bucquet and Gingembre, also advised me
My knowledge of chemistry enabled me to be a laboratory assistant
The work was exciting and interesting
My role, initially, was to draw sketches of the work
Training from the painter Jacques-Louis David was helpful
My knowledge of English and Latin was useful to make translations
Kirwan's *Essay on Phlogiston* was one example
Antoine, as a result, developed oxygen gas

I translated English works by Priestley and also Cavendish
Gradually, my role became more important
It involved project co-ordination in the laboratory
In 1789, we put together a major work
Lavoisier's Elementary Treatise on Chemistry
13 of my drawings were included
In addition, my notes on the experiments were used
These were to prove invaluable
Disaster was about to strike
The French Revolution began in 1789
Revolutionaries created a reign of terror
We lived in fear of our lives
Antoine was a member of the *Ferme Generale*
It was the organisation that collected taxes for the old regime
The revolutionaries attacked all those involved
A false charge was that Antoine aided foreign scientists
He was arrested in 1793, and accused of being a traitor
My father was also arrested in May 1794
I visited and made representations to have them released
Enemies like Dupin refused to listen or take action
I stressed Antoine's great work as a scientist and chemist
It made no impression
One of the judges said, 'We do not need scientists or chemists'
'The course of justice cannot be delayed'
On May 8th 1794, my husband, aged 51, was led to the guillotine
23 years of happy marriage died with him
My father was also executed on the same day
Darkness descended on my life
The new Government lackeys were vicious in their reprisals
All of my money and property were confiscated
They also seized my husband's notebooks and equipment
Despite the despair, I knew his life should not be in vain
It became my objective to publish my husband's research
With difficulty, I regained as many documents as possible
The book *Memoires de Chimie* was eventually published
The first volume contained his work on heat and liquids
The second book was on combustion, metals, acids and water
My preface praised my husband's achievements

Equally, I attacked his murderers
Maybe for safety reasons, the printers did not include it
The works of Antoine Lavoisier became famous
Securing his legacy was no less than he deserved
An innovator and hard worker, he led the way
The French revolutionaries cut down a French hero

Who knows what other great work he would have produced?
After the Revolution, a new Government took over
A note with my husband's belongings was sent to me
'To the widow of Lavoisier who was falsely convicted'
Still in my thirties, I had to start again
It was difficult for, as a woman, I could not practice science

It was seen as the preserve of men
There were too many prejudices and barriers
Yet, I did not want a menial job, or just to be left in the house
I felt the need for company
In due course, other men came into my life
Pierre Samuel du Pont de Nemours was one
He proposed marriage, but I decided against it
After about ten years, I met another scientist
Benjamin Thompson, an American, was five years older than me
We shared an interest in science
A leading physicist, he helped found The Royal Institution
As an inventor, he developed the wax candle and Rumford Soup
He proposed a number of times during our four year courtship
Eventually, in 1805, I consented and we married
It was a decision that I regretted
The marriage lasted only a short time
Once again, I was on my own
A time to reflect on my life with Antoine
People continued to refer to me as Madame Lavoisier
It was an honour
Reflecting a decision I made at the age of 13
A decision made under pressure
It was a decision that I never regretted.

Augusta Ada Lovelace
1815–1852

My father was Lord Byron, the celebrated poet
However, I did not know him
He left my mother and I when I was five months old
That was the last time he saw me
In between writing, he was away having affairs and breakdowns
He died when I was eight years old
My mother, Annabella, ensured that I had a sound education
She chose mathematics and music as two key topics
Her view was that they were good subjects for training the mind
It was unusual for girls to receive tuition
There was no public education system in England at that time
Therefore, most people did not go to school
In particular, it was widely thought education was wasted on girls
It was expected that they should marry and look after children
It was an unwritten rule that men were in control
Women should not 'interfere' in politics, religion or business
It was assumed that women should know their place
Despite this, my mother arranged private tuition
Miss Lamont was my first teacher
Geography was a subject that I enjoyed
Mother objected and replaced one of the lessons with arithmetic
She had a strong view on what was good for me
Although she decided my studies, we were not close
Her other activities took up a great deal of her time
Many tutors were appointed and I had to work hard
Some family members said it was too much work
They wanted me to have more time to play
Mother ignored them and gave me punishments if I did not do well
Solitary confinement and having to stay motionless were two examples
Also, she demanded that I write apologies over small matters
By the age of 14, I was feeling under pressure
A peculiar illness came upon me
For three years, I lost the ability to walk properly
Confined to the house, I continued with my studies

Augusta Lovelace

During this time I became an accomplished musician
Also, I had tuition in foreign languages
Mathematics, however, was my main subject
There was a beauty and elegance to the formulae and equations
The book *The Mechanism of the Heavens* impressed me
Written by Mary Somerville, it dealt with mathematical astronomy
As a result, we met and became friends
In 1832, she introduced me to Lord William King
A very clever man, he became one of my tutors
Aged 27, he was ten years older than me
Although young, I was attracted to him
When I was 20, we married and had three children
He became an Earl in 1838 and took the title 'Earl Lovelace'
That is how I became known as Ada Lovelace
It was a life of high society, meeting influential people
David Brewster, developer of the kaleidoscope, was one
Also, I met Charles Dickens and other writers
Scientists, like Charles Wheatstone and Michael Faraday, visited
At dinner, they shared their ideas
Mrs Somerville was also very helpful in other ways
She invited me to a dinner party at her home in 1834
Discussion centred on Charles Babbage's work
What I heard fascinated me
He was developing a new calculating engine
This challenged my thinking about the future of mathematics
We met and he outlined his grand plans for a computer
With my knowledge of mathematics, we had a lot in common
I understood better than most people what he was doing
We continued to talk and share ideas
In 1841, Babbage went to Turin, Italy, and gave a talk on his work
Luigi Menabrea was there and wrote an article on the key points
A copy of this was given to me
With my linguistic ability, I was able to translate it into English
Babbage was delighted and suggested that I add my own notes
It ended up three times the length of the original
In the document, I outlined how Babbage's machine could be used
My view was that it had greater potential than just a calculating machine
I proposed that it be used to compose music and produce graphics

In addition, I advocated its use in science and other practical purposes
The document was signed simply with my initials
It was unbecoming for a lady of my class to put her full name on it
My view, reflective of the time, was that it was 'unfeminine'
Babbage felt it should be published and made the arrangements
It appeared in Richard Taylor's *Scientific Memoirs* in 1843
My discussions with Charles Babbage continued
They focused on mathematical applications
In particular, I developed an algorithm to calculate Bernoulli numbers
That became the foundation for the first computer program
It was a pity that we did not have more time to work together
So many people ignored or derided his great work
They did not have the vision to appreciate his breakthrough
He never wrote an article on his work
Practical demonstration was his forte
Writing things down was mine and we made a good team
I witnessed the development of Babbage's engine with pleasure
It was designed to read and store data and perform basic calculations
The start of a revolution in the management of information
The world of the calculating machine and the computer
Yet, our work relationship was short-lived
Once again, I was having problems with my health
My energy began to ebb away
Medication was prescribed, but did not resolve the problems
Doctors were called and more treatments tried
None of them worked and I was confined to the house
It became clear that I was suffering from a cancer
At the age of 37, amidst tears, I said goodbye to my children and husband
Requesting in my Will to be buried beside my father
The father that I had never met
Yet I hoped that my spirit, like his, would live on.

Post Script
In 1979, Ada Lovelace's work was recognised
A new computer language was commissioned, based on Pascal
The United States Department of Defence called it ADA
A brand for professional recognition
A credit to the work done with Charles Babbage.

Elizabeth Macarthur
1766–1850

I chose to go to Australia with convicts
We set sail on a cold winter's day from England
There were six ships in the fleet, carrying 939 male convicts
In addition, there were 78 women convicted of crime
All sentenced for deportation to the Great Southern Land
It was my sentence also, as I volunteered to go with my husband
He was an Army Captain, charged with keeping law and order
It was an horrific journey, over mountainous seas
Days of squalor and terror, as the sailors abused the convicts
There was widespread disease in the damp and dismal conditions
Boredom prevailed, riding the ocean waves day after day
Agony for the convicts, who were kept below the decks
Sailing to an unknown land, in a ship that did well to stay afloat
Added to the problems was my pregnancy on the high seas
Tragically, my daughter died soon after birth
Therefore, I was in a state of depression for a long time
My other child, Edward, born in 1788, was fortunate to survive
Arriving in June 1790, at Sydney Town, I hoped for better times
What I found shocked me
The people on the First Fleet of 1788 had survived, but only just
Poverty, sickness and filth lay all around
I did not want to stay, but could not return to England
The settlers and convicts were in a dreadful state
Indeed, the aborigines seemed to live better
At least, they had learnt how to live on this island
The colonists were delighted to see us
They asked so many questions, seeking news from home
But, we also brought problems
Six ships had set sail, but only five arrived
The ship with our provisions, *The Guardian,* did not make it
So many mouths to feed and so little food
It had been a voyage of despair
Also, at least 278 people died *en route,* and more on landing
It was a time of great sadness and desolation on the ocean

Elizabeth Macarthur

Many convicts brought disease, for they were severely ill
Most had been mistreated and starved
We arrived aboard the *Scarborough*
The voyage, which seemed like a lifetime, had taken six months
My immediate task was to help organise places to live
It was like an open-air mad house
I wrote that it was "a sink of evil already …
And more like a gypsy encampment than part of a town"
Many of the new arrivals had contagious diseases
Scurvy, dysentery, typhoid fever and smallpox were rife

We did not even know the names of some of the illnesses
Nor did we have medicine to alleviate the suffering
The existing settlers did not have facilities to cope
No one had planned for this type of chaos
The British Government had cast aside its convicts and citizens

There was a lot to do
Once established, I focused on our family life
Gradually, we were able to move to the countryside
In 1793, we were allocated 100 acres of land
It meant that I had to learn the skills of managing an estate
We had convicts to help us clear the land
Later, we were allocated another 100 acres
Located at Parramatta, we called it Elizabeth Farm
By 1796, we had between 400 and 500 acres
Much wheat was grown, as well as fruit and vegetables
My husband was frequently absent
Although a soldier, he was by nature an entrepreneur
His work took him to Sydney and overseas
In 1796, he returned with Merino sheep from South Africa
They were suited to the hard arid land
Within a few years, we had 4000 sheep
After ten years, we had established ourselves
I wrote, "Nothing induces me to wish for a change
… but the difficulty of educating our children"
In 1801, John returned to England on business
He took with him two of my dear children, to be educated
From that time until 1805 when he returned, I fended for myself
Hard work in the sun and lonely nights
The sheep farm prospered
The wool produced was of a high quality
John had made arrangements for us to sell it in England
In 1807, we sent the first exports to our home country
In the meantime, John made enemies in the colony
Also, he was involved in the illegal rum trade
In particular, my husband clashed with Governor Bligh
The man that had created mutiny on the *Bounty* ship
Tempers flared and another mutiny rose up against him
John was sent to England for a court martial
Our youngest son also went with him to be educated
During that time, I consolidated the work that we had begun
John wrote to say our sons were in public school
Also, after investigation, he had not been arrested
My husband continued to develop business contacts

It was a long time before I saw him again
Once again, I was left to fend for myself and family
I managed the estate alone from 1809 to 1817
Surrounded by convict slave labour and aborigines
All of whom helped me in various ways
The climate was harsh and the living was never easy
The demand for wool increased and our wealth with it
In 1815 alone, I sold 15,000 pounds of wool

Expansion led to three locations for production
It was a considerable task to manage all three centres
Elizabeth Farm, Seven Hills Farm and Camden Park Estates
Prior to John's absences, we had started a family
In all, I had eight children, and six survived infancy
My daughter Emmeline arrived when I was 42
I was their breadwinner, teacher and mother

But, I had to send the boys to England for their education
The girls stayed with me
Entertainment was scarce and the nights long
Only candles relieved the evening gloom
But, during the day I kept very busy
Thanks to Dr Worgon, I had the first piano in the colony
I tried to learn how to play it
When my husband returned in 1817, we started to produce wine
It was the start of another testing period
He suffered a mental breakdown and I nursed him
Beset by melancholy and fears, he was much tormented
We continued to develop the farm but in 1834, aged 68, he died
Despite the separations and problems, we had achieved a great deal
Most important was helping our new nation develop
In doing so, we established agriculture and commerce
We had convict labour to assist and Government land
Beyond that, we had determination
Plus, the ability to learn from our actions
Those, above all, were the factors that enabled us to survive
After John's death, I continued on
Helping the new generation build their lives in the colony
Seeing the end of convict ships and the arrival of more free settlers
Living to the grand age of 86
A founding mother of a new country.

Golda Meir
1898–1978

Fear was a major part of my early life
I remember my father boarding up our front door
He had heard that Jews were about to be attacked
Pogroms was the Russian word for violence against a group
We lived near Kiev in the Russian Empire
Jews were often persecuted there and elsewhere
The historical cross that we bore
We were never sure when our home would be attacked
Not that it was grand and worth attacking
My father was a lumberman and we lived in poor circumstances
Winters were very cold and we were often hungry
Adding to my fears was the fact that five of my siblings died
As I was struggling to survive, death visited our house regularly
My other sisters, Sheyna and Tzipke, therefore kept very close
In 1903, my father left home to search for a better life in the USA
He said that he would earn enough money, so that we could follow
It took him three years
In 1906, my mother, Blume, took us across the Atlantic
A rough shipboard journey, full of promise, to a new land
Little did we know the problems that faced us
None of us spoke English, or understood the culture
We lived in Milwaukee, where Father was a carpenter
My mother established a grocery store
I helped each morning, while she was at the market
After that, I went to the Fourth Street School
One of my classmates was very poor and did not have textbooks
I formed a group to help raise money for her
My beliefs in helping the under-privileged had begun to show
However, I needed help myself
Aged 14, I did part-time work after school
My mother felt that I should cease going to school and get married
Fear once again rose inside me and I ran away to Denver
My older sister Sheyna lived there and took me in for a year
I continued my education at North High School

Golda Meir

Despite my mother's concerns, it was there that I met my husband
Morris Meyerson was a student and we married in 1917
I was only 19 years of age
Nevertheless, I was not going to stay at home
Politics interested me and I joined various groups
In 1915, I became a member of the Labor Zionist Organisation
Having such strong views, it was natural that I wanted to make *aliyah*
That is the term we used for emigration to the Land of Israel
At that time, it was part of the Ottoman Empire
Battles raged for the control of the land
It was the Arabs that pushed them out, not the Jewish people
To us, it was an ancestral home land
In 1921, my husband, Sheyna and I emigrated to Palestine
We settled in Tel Aviv, which was under a British Mandate
We lived on a *kibbutz* and had two children, Sarah and Menachem
Later we moved to Jerusalem
It was a testing time, as we again learnt to adapt
Living and working conditions were poor and life was hard
I pressed for social change in a practical way
In 1928, I became a leader of the Women's Labor Council
It involved helping women find and retain work
It included a representation role in the USA from 1932 to 1934
On returning to Palestine, I was asked to join the Histadrut
This was a top level union role, in a key political organisation
On reflection, it put a great strain on our family
The children stayed with my husband, as I returned to Tel Aviv
The Histadrut evolved to become the shadow government
We wanted a new country called Israel
Internationally, there were larger battles taking place
The Second World War meant that all efforts had to be focused on that
In Europe, Germans were killing millions of people
In particular, they targeted Jews
They murdered over 6,000,000 in their gas chambers
The Russians were also organising *pogroms* and persecuting Jews
It was a fight for our existence and we put our effort behind the allies
After the war, our battle continued
The British opposed the Zionist movement in Palestine
My role was to negotiate with them

Behind me was a guerilla group taking direct action
After a mighty struggle, it was agreed that we should have our own land
I was one of the 24 people to sign the Israeli Declaration of Independence
A day of joy, a dream come true
Yet, all around, there were threats, particularly from Jordan
I made a dangerous journey in disguise to see their King
He refused to make peace and attacked our new country
Also joined by Iraq, Egypt, and Syria

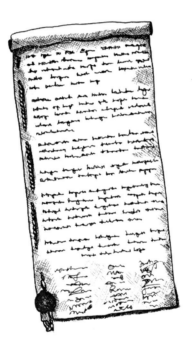

Declaration of Israeli Independence

The Arab Israeli War commenced
I went to the USA to raise funds
Meanwhile, our brave fighters saved our new nation
Now, we had to build international links
I was asked to be the Israeli Ambassador to Russia
Moscow was a cold place in more senses than one

Stalin had repressed our people, but Russian Jews welcomed me
On my return, I was elected to our Parliament, the Knesset
Serving the people as an elected member from 1949 to 1974
Initially as Labour Minister and then Foreign Minister
Ben Gurian, our Prime Minister, proposed that I take a Hebrew name

I chose Meir, meaning 'to illuminate', and became known as Golda Meir
Work was hard and relentless
I began to feel tired and was diagnosed with lymphoma
It led to my resignation from the Cabinet in 1965

Over time, my health improved
In 1969 I was asked to be Prime Minister
It was a tumultuous time
Israel had recently won the so called Arab-Israeli Six Day War
Large areas of new territory had been captured
It was the start of many new developments
We had to build up our industries and trade internationally
People wanted a better standard of life
We needed money to buy new weapons and defend ourselves
Including nuclear weapons, which we succeeded in developing
At the same time, we opened the doors to Jews from many countries
Giving others the chance that I had taken in 1924
Yet, there were many sad days, not least in September 1972
Arab terrorists murdered 11 of our Olympic Team at Munich
Once again Jews being killed on German soil
Diplomacy was always top of my agenda
Trying to gain support in the USA and Europe, in particular
Recognising that war was always on our doorstep
It flared up again, in 1973, with the Yom Kippur War
The Arab countries attacked the Golan Heights and Sinai
The Russians supplied them with weapons
European countries refused to help us
I appealed to the USA, as it was a matter of life or death
President Nixon, to his credit, authorised military support
Portugal provided a staging post for re-fuelling and supplies
Just in time to help us defeat the enemy
The result was that Arab states declared an oil embargo on the USA
The 1973 oil crisis rocked the world economies
Israel survived, but at a huge cost internally and externally
I was 73 years of age and younger people needed to lead the nation
In 1974, I resigned, having been called 'The Iron Lady'
However, my body was not made of iron and my health suffered
My move from Russia to the USA and Israel had been for a purpose
Happily, I saw my five grandchildren grow up
Living in a country governed by Jewish people
They and others inherited Israel, a place for Jews to live
A purpose that had to continue with a new generation at the helm.

Maria Montessori
1870–1952

My mother stressed it was important to be compassionate
Each day, she asked me to knit some clothing for the poor
There were a lot of poor people near our home
We lived in Chiaravalle, Italy
Fortunately, my family could afford to send me to school
My father was a retired army officer
He had a traditional approach to the role of women
An arranged marriage was his view of my future
He wanted me to leave school, not pursue a career
Mother supported my further education
When I was 14 years of age, I enrolled at a technical institute
In effect, it was a school for boys, as few girls applied
Initially, my interest was in mathematics and engineering
Learning about biology changed my focus
It gave me a purpose
I decided to be a doctor
Easier said than done in Italy
It was a man's world, dominated by three organisations:
The Roman Catholic Church, the Mafia and the Government
No woman had ever qualified to enter the medical profession
It was a challenge even to gain entry and be treated as an equal
Male colleagues felt that a woman's place was in the home
'Equal opportunities for all' was my motto
By 1894, after much hard work, I qualified
The first woman in Italy to gain a medical degree
My first job was at a psychiatric clinic at Rome University
Most of the training had been on clinical and surgical issues
Both on curing and preventing
Pasteur's new germ theory was becoming accepted
The main focus had been on physical ailments
Little had been said about mental problems
We had few tools to treat those with such disabilities
The children did not have broken bones
Nor did they have diseases in the conventional sense

Maria Montessori

Yet, they had difficulty communicating and coping
In my personal life, I also had difficulties
Through my work, I met an interesting man
The relationship led from walks and talks to the bedroom
Of course, I knew the risks
Nevertheless, it was a shock when I found that I was pregnant
In 1898, I gave birth to my son
For various reasons, marriage was not possible
That meant major problems for me and my family
An unmarried mother in Catholic Italy meant social exclusion
My parents thought it best to arrange an adoption
Days and nights of anguish
What was the right thing to do?
The pressure on me was strong
Therefore, I agreed to the adoption
It was to be another 15 years before I saw my son, Mario
In 1898, I was appointed to a new role
Director of the State Orthophrenic School in Rome
Its declared mission was to care for the 'hopelessly deficient'
Some people called the children 'idiots' or 'lunatics'
All of them had problems communicating and relating
Therefore, I questioned was this just a medical task?
The greater task was an educational one
Could the 'hopelessly deficient', and so called 'idiots', learn?
That became my challenge each day
Slowly, we made progress in practical ways
It was no use giving talks and lectures
Each child needed to be shown what to do
Simple things, like washing and making their beds
Essential things, like eating and cleaning up afterwards
The staff had to help the students to learn by doing
Demonstration, action and then repetition
The same applied when it came to play
The children had not learnt how to play games
Again, the practical approach helped them
By 1901, I had established this new approach and moved on
It was time to conduct further study and research
However, my reputation for helping the disabled followed me

In 1906, the government asked me to work in another school
There were 60 children from poverty-stricken families
This time, it was education first, rather than medicine
Rather than teach, I focused on creating a learning atmosphere
Small tables were provided, rather than rows of desks
Encouragement, rather than threats and punishment, was given
Helping children experiment, rather than just comply
Our *Casa dei Bambini* enabled the children to learn by doing
My job was to help the staff create the materials
They included counting beads and geometric puzzles

Learning time was play time
Play time was learning time
The important thing was to help children to have success
Encouraging and rewarding achievement was vital
Other educators wondered what we were doing
They asked, when would we follow the curriculum?
Their focus was on teaching
Ours was on learning, via demonstration and practice
In particular, enabling one child to help another
Helping them to learn how to develop relationships

Developing the senses, as a base for developing the intellect
It was all rewarding work, yet I could not forget my own son
We had not met, but I wanted to know him
Enquiries were made
Mario, aged 15, was told I was his mother
In 1913, I was reunited with him
A day of great happiness
News of my educational approach went beyond Rome
In 1915, I was invited to the USA
Mario accompanied me on the ship across the Atlantic Ocean
Hours in which to talk, and get to know each other
We agreed, that in public, I should refer to him as my nephew
Inappropriate gossip needed to be avoided
In New York, I spoke at the Carnegie Hall
Thomas Edison was interested in my ideas and met me
Alexander Graham Bell sponsored my approach
He became President of the American Montessori Society
His wife, who was deaf, liked my educational approach
In San Francisco, I established a 'Montessori classroom'
It was good to see the American people were interested
In reality, the whole of America was a Montessori classroom
It was a land of opportunity, where many learned by doing
However, it was hit and miss, without guidance and support
Across the Atlantic came bad news
In Europe, the First World War killed millions
Destruction beyond imagination
Denying a generation the opportunity to develop their potential
Children had their infancy stolen from them
Young men lost their lives
During the 1920s and 1930s, I continued with my work
In 1922, I became Inspector of Schools in Italy
International interest followed
In 1929, the *Association Montessori Internationale* was started
Encouraging parents and teachers to help their children learn
My son, Mario, joined me in my work
He became my greatest supporter
His efforts to spread the message were tireless
Yet, I feared that war would return

There was mass unemployment and poverty
Fascism and Nazism reared their ugly heads
I voiced my opposition to Mussolini, the Italian Fascist leader
Dissent was not allowed
It became necessary to move to Spain
While there, I introduced my educational approach
A chance also to learn Spanish, using my own methods
Then, in 1936, the destructive Spanish Civil War began
Relocating to the Netherlands, I continued my work
It was a chance to introduce my ideas in a new language
Albert Max Joosten joined, and worked with me for many years
In 1939, an invitation to India proved valuable
The Theosophical Society wanted to introduce my approach
Mario went with me, and we lived in Adyar, Chennai
During our stay, the Germans invaded the Netherlands
We therefore stayed in India and conducted 16 courses
The war changed our lives
Sadly, as we were still Italian citizens, we were interned
On our release, we created Indian Montessori Training Courses
The war at that time dominated people's thoughts
Once it was over, we sighed with relief
India was an amazing country
Likewise Pakistan, where I ran some courses
Our education programmes would help future generations
In Italy, I was honoured in 1947
In Rome, Opera Montessori, was named after me
In 1949, I returned to the Netherlands
Aged 79, I realised the need to plan for the future
More time was given to our coordinating organisation
The *Association Montessori Internationale*
Albert Max Joosten became my trusted representative
Working to develop our international schools
'Educate for Peace'
That, I believed, was the key principle
It resulted in three nominations for the Nobel Peace Prize
The education of children was the most important thing
The processes were well-tried, and worked in every country
That was my legacy and may it continue.

Mother Teresa
1910–1997

My family came from Shkoder, Albania
I was born in a poor area near Skopje
My parents had strong beliefs and were involved in politics
Sadly, my father collapsed and died when I was eight
Mother took me to the Roman Catholic Church
There, I learned about missionaries and their service to others
At the age of 12, I decided to be a missionary
It required a devotion to the religious life
Aged 18, I said goodbye to my mother and sister
I never saw them again
It was a decision for a lifetime
No boyfriends, no husband, no children
Committed only to the service of Christ
Joining the Sisters of Loreto at Rathfarnham, Ireland, in 1928
The first task was to learn English
A year later, another culture shock, arriving in Darjeeling, India
A realization of what missionary work is really like
Poverty was all around
After two years, I took my first religious vows
Changing my name to Sister Teresa
In respect of Therese de Lisieux, patron saint of missionaries
It was the beginning of a task without end
Moving to Calcutta was disturbing
So many people existing in shacks
Children begging on the streets
Illness and injuries and few medical facilities
My role was to teach at the Loreto Convent School
Guiding the more privileged and preaching mostly to converts
The vast majority of Indians followed different religions
Leading to violence and death between Hindus, Sikhs and Muslims
Undeterred, I pursued my vocation and took my vows in 1937
Looking to God for guidance to help those in the gutters
The Second World War resulted in more privations
The famine of 1943 brought more death

Mother Teresa

These sights and experiences influenced my prayers
Then came the 'call within the call'
To me, it was an Order from God
I was to leave the convent and help the poor
To do this meant living among them
In 1948, I changed my dress to a white cotton chira with a blue border
My destination was the slums of Motijhil
Practical help, rather than just prayer, was needed
Finding food and shelter for the destitute and starving
Like many of the poor, I had no income
So, begging for supplies and help became a way of life
A free nun covered by the poverty of the cross
Word of my efforts reached the Indian Prime Minister
The Vatican also took note
They approved a congregation called Missionaries of Charity
Approval and application are two different things
The task was to care for the hungry, the naked and the homeless
Also, the crippled, the blind, the lepers and the unloved and unwanted
We started with a small group of thirteen
It grew to an organization of 4,000 nuns
We managed orphanages, hospices and refugee centres in many places
Victims of floods, famine and epidemics arrived
The blind, aged, disabled and alcoholics were our companions
In 1952, I helped establish a Home for the Dying
Kalighat, Home of the Pure of Heart, is the name we gave it
All faiths were welcome
Next, a home called City of Peace was opened for lepers
This led to community clinics being established elsewhere
People and officials started to assist
Hospices, orphanages and leper houses were open in many Indian cities
The missionary work then expanded to other countries
To Venezuela in 1965 and to Italy, Tanzania and Austria in 1968
During the 1970s, our work spread to Asia, Africa and the USA
Nuns, assisted by volunteers, did amazing work to help those in need
Criticisms, of course, were made
It was said that we kept people alive
But, we failed to tackle the causes of poverty
Some said the quality of medical care was not sufficient

No doubt improvements could have been made
Our practice was driven by the needs of the people and our convictions
Action often came first and learning second, accommodating the demand
At the age of 72, I was called again, this time to Beirut
Thirty-seven children were between the Israeli and Palestinian fighters
With the help of the Red Cross, we evacuated the children
Then came opportunities in Eastern Europe to help the poor
Communism was in decline and the Church could do its work
Practical Christian faith was replacing Marxist dogma
More work was needed in Africa and I went to Ethiopia
Then to Armenia and Russia to assist earthquake and radiation victims
At last, in 1991, I returned to Albania
A Missionaries of Charity Brothers was established in Tirana
Around the world, we had 517 missions in more than 100 countries
En route, I survived a heart attack in 1983 and another in 1989
Time was against me, but our work continued on
Over 4,000 nuns were dedicated to the work
In addition, there were over 300 in the brotherhood
Lay volunteer workers numbered over 100,000
Many honours were awarded to me
Including the Nobel Peace Prize in 1979
The real honour was to have helped those in need
In particular, to have fulfilled my calling in the name of the Church
Following also the philosophy of St Francis of Assisi
Poverty, chastity, obedience and submission to Christ
My focus was to use these strengths to help people
So that they could join the Catholic Church and be blessed
Knowing that, as Christians, they could be saved
They called me Mother Teresa
Though I had no children, I saved many.

Florence Nightingale
1820–1910

From the age of 17, I knew my destiny lay with many men
I said 'no' to the proposals of marriage that I received
I felt strongly that my role in life was to help others
Beyond my education in Latin, Greek, German, French and Italian
My first name came from the city of Florence in Italy
That is where I was born
My parents came from a well-endowed English family
They were disappointed and upset when I chose to be a nurse
This occupation was seen by my parents as a menial type of work
Also, I worked to improve the Poor Laws in England
In 1837, God spoke to me and called me to his service
Too many people were caught in the poverty trap
On a visit to Kaiserwerth, Germany, I saw higher standards of care
It showed me that I could help improve nursing standards
On returning, Richard Monkton Milnes, an MP, courted me
He proposed marriage, but I had to say no
My parents again did not approve of my actions
It was stressful, and I put distance between us by going to Rome
There, I felt depressed
During my stay I met Sidney Herbert, another politician
Although he was married, he became a close friend and supporter
In 1850, my family sent me to Egypt due to further health problems
On this visit, God spoke to me about my life and his work
It led me to write in my diary some personal notes
'Today I am 30, the age Christ began his mission
No more childish things
No more love
No more marriage
Now Lord, let me think only of Thy Will'
So, the decision was made
In 1851, I returned to Kaiserwerth, Germany, to train as a nurse
Again, my parents strongly objected
Whilst there, I had an intense divine calling
In 1853, I returned to care for sick women in London

Florence Nightingale

My father supported me with an income despite his concerns
Henry Manning, a Catholic priest, helped and became a friend
At this time, I heard of the Crimea War atrocities
I knew that I must assist our injured men at the front
In October 1854, I organised some volunteers
With 38 other female nurses, I went to Scutari ,Turkey
There, I witnessed the appalling conditions of the wounded
Many dying unnecessarily for the want of attention
Typhus, cholera, dysentery and gangrene added to their injuries of battle
Military doctors in the main scorned our arrival
They made our work more difficult
We pressed for some changes and began work
Basic nursing, such as washing wounds and hygiene reduced infection
I did not know Dr Semmelweis in Vienna was fighting such ignorance
It was a battle within the battle
Too many good men died by neglect
I was amazed by the lack of concern doctors had for post-operative care
With no antibiotics, there was a limit to our medication
We tried to keep infection at bay by simple means
Washing patients and putting on clean bandages were the main ones
It was said that I was the 'lady with the lamp'
Tending the sick late at night
However, 4077 soldiers died during our first winter there
I gathered statistics to provide evidence
The sewers were a source for disease, and later improved
Ten times the number of soldiers died from infection after battle
At that time, the medical world was divided on the cause of infection
Lister, Pasteur, Koch and bacterial analysis were 20 and 30 years away
We battled on with belief, if not always enough evidence
On my return from the Fields of Hell on Earth, I also became ill
Probably a disease from the Crimea that restricted me to my room
However, my work was not forgotten
Queen Victoria, via Sidney Herbert, asked my advice on health issues
A Royal Commission led me to write the report of more than 1000 pages
It required most of my time and energy
Again evidence was hard to obtain
But, it was clear that a prevention strategy was better than a cure
The Sanitary Commission of 1857 demanded clean water

I noted the work of Dr Snow and his attack on cholera
Prevention of disease was essential
Hygiene and cleanliness in hospitals was my cry
It was hard to believe that so many people ignored it
Therefore, I established more statistical records

That led me to become President of the Royal Statistical Society in 1858
I also wrote two books in 1859 on nursing and hospitals
To improve the work of the profession, I raised 59,000 pounds
With that money, I pressed for more and better training

The Nightingale School of Nursing in London was opened in 1860
That helped provide qualified nurses to many parts of the country
To guide them, I wrote *Notes on Nursing* in 1860
I also campaigned for women's rights and career opportunities
There was opposition from many
They said, 'A woman's place was in the home'
My place was in the field of battle to improve health and women's rights
Firstly as a nurse, and then as an administrator
In addition, my work as a researcher and writer helped the cause

The Florence Nightingale Medal

Raising money, and the spirits of those in need, was important
With Elizabeth Blackwell, I opened a Women's Medical College in 1869
It involved a lot of political work to influence people
Many listened, but most took no action
Some were openly hostile, and some apathetic
Only a few really supported our efforts

Benjamin Jowett became a special friend
He helped me through some dark times
It was hard to keep going against apathy in high places
Gradually, the importance of good nursing practice was recognised
Doctors in hospitals were often the hardest people to convince
Government officials were often slow to support with public money
However, by the time I was 65, I could see progress
Many awards, including the Royal Red Cross, were given to me
I continued to press for reform, until 1895 when I became blind
However, I kept a close interest in developments
The work of Semmelweis, Pasteur, Koch and Lister became known
They were heroes in the fight against bacterial infection
Enabling nurses to become heroines
They applied the research by improving hygiene to keep people alive
The status, if not the pay, of nurses, was rising
Yet, another war was soon to follow
Again, so many died, both on the field and in hospitals
The lessons of sanitation and nursing care were still being learned.
That battle will go on forever.

Emmeline Pankhurst
1858–1928

I was arrested by the police many times
They locked me up and treated me like a common convict
Labelled as 'dangerous'
My so-called crime was to fight for women's rights
In late 19th Century England, women were second-class citizens
They had no vote
Restrictions were placed on what work women could do
Education facilities for girls were poor
Medical advice on women's health was almost non-existent
In the cities, and villages, widespread poverty existed
The average life span of a woman was about 50 years
Children were left without mothers and husbands without wives
I felt compelled to improve the conditions
As an educated person, it was my duty to fight for women's rights
Born at Stretford, Lancashire, I saw the realities every day
Women trying to bring up their children in dilapidated houses
Disease from poor sanitation all around
Dependent, mainly, on their men folk for income
Many of whom were on low wages and irregular work
Too many unemployed and depressed
Too often, family income was spent on drink
From an early age, I realised that political action was needed
My parents were social reform activists
Education to them was a right
At the age of 15, I was sent to Paris and gained a wider view
Liberty, Fraternity and Equality is what the French believed
Despite the revolution, the French fell short on human rights
Women did not have the same opportunities as men
On returning to England, I realised action was needed
Democracy meant that men and women should have equal rights
Yet, Parliament was full of men
So was the House of Lords
Ironically, our Head of State was a woman, Queen Victoria
When I was born, she had been on the throne 20 years

Emmeline Pankhurst

Victoria seemed more interested in her Empire
Rights for women in her own country were ignored
By the time I married, the Queen had been in power 40 years
Still, women did not have equal political rights with men
One man, however, firmly believed in equal rights
Meeting Richard Pankhurst was a turning point in my life
He was 45 years old and I was only 20
Trained as a lawyer, he had campaigned for women's rights
That was most unusual

He had written *The Married Women's Property Acts*
We shared our ideas and ideals
Despite the age gap, we fell in love and married in 1879
Family was important to us and we had five children
Sadly, two of my sons died during infancy
With my husband, I campaigned continually for human rights
Particularly, political rights for women
For nearly 20 years, we worked together on this issue

During this time, he complained of stomach pains
Gastric ulcers were diagnosed, but could not be cured
On July 5th 1898, my daughters and I were distraught at his death
We resolved to carry on with our campaign
That is what he would have wanted
My daughters grew up to be women's rights activists
Christabel and Sylvia were tireless workers in the cause
Adela emigrated to Australia and joined political groups
My focus was on getting democracy to work in Britain
In 1903, we formed the Women's Social and Political Union (WSPU)
It was the 'suffrage army in the field'
Christabel, our eldest daughter, became a leading strategist
Her bold action led to her imprisonment
Sylvia, our second daughter, was an artist and created banners
We held public meetings and marches
It provided the focus point for women to rally
Torchlight processions and colourful events were our trademark
When any WSPU member was in prison, we protested
When they were released, we had grand street parade celebrations
It was important to have a theatre of civil rights
We paraded in silk petticoats
Matrons with 'hammers' marched the streets
Ladies held up stones in kid gloves
These were not empty stunts
They were part of our democratic rights
We paraded and protested to show we meant business
If democracy meant anything, we had the right to have our say
Men in black suits were in our way
They sat in Parliament, opposing us with long speeches
They sat in Courts, judging us and sending us to prison
The police and jailors did their bidding
Bureaucrats supported them by being obstructive
The system fostered a conspiracy against women's rights
Direct action to change things was necessary
Some of our members resorted to breaking the law
Arson, smashing windows and destruction of property occurred
Some of our members chained themselves to fences
Others took the fight to racecourses and the doors of the rich

We had to use all social and political avenues
Some saw it as the battle of the sexes
Others saw our protests as a kind of civil war
To me it was always the battle for civil rights
The movement gathered strength and became more violent
In 1910, I was arrested and put in prison 12 times
Men called me a 'rabble rouser'
At times, I was force fed after going on a hunger strike
They addressed me formally as Mrs Pankhurst
Privately, those men in high places derided me as a mischief-maker
In Court, I regularly spoke my mind
'We are here not as law breakers, we are here to become law makers'
That was a message I repeated time after time
The male-dominated legal profession closed their ears and eyes
So did the male politicians, but not the popular newspapers
In 1910, with colleagues, I led a protest to Prime Minister Asquith
The Conciliation Bill, giving us the vote, was being dropped
To his shame, Asquith refused to see our delegation
Police stopped our entry into Parliament
A riot ensued and over 100 women were arrested
We called it 'Black Friday'
It felt as if we were about to have a civil war
However, another war with incredible consequences was starting
The Kaiser and his German army were on the march through Europe
The First World War commenced and killing on a colossal scale began
Our nation needed to be united
Women were required in the factories and on the land
Women were needed as nurses in hospitals, to tend the wounded
We agreed to suspend the suffragette campaign
All our imprisoned sisters were released
I visited the USA, Canada and Russia to encourage women
Again, I found male-dominated politics restricting them
There was a need to spell out the new agenda
My Own Story, published in 1914, outlined my experiences
In 1917, our movement became The Women's Party
By 1918, the vote for women aged over 30 had been secured
It was progress and we celebrated the end of the war
Women had contributed in a major way to the military victory

It was, however, only a partial political victory
Women had to have a property qualification
However, all men of 21 years and above could vote
So much for equality!
Aged 60, my role needed to be transferred to younger women
I went to live in the USA, Canada and also Bermuda
On returning to England in 1926, I decided to run for Parliament
The Conservatives chose me as their candidate
Ill health prevented me from having the opportunity

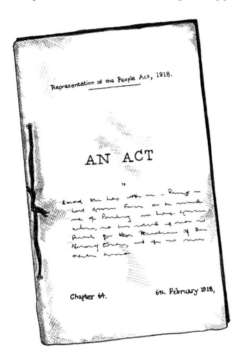

The new Parliament, however, addressed the key question
Equal votes for women and men
The Representation of the People Act was passed
We had achieved our main political goal
It was just in time, as I was very ill
But, there was a new agenda for the next generation
Women had the vote, but not equal employment rights
There was still a lot to do.

Eva Peron
1919–1952

Growing up poor is no sin
But, it has little virtue
My parents were not married
In Catholic Argentina, it felt as if I had sinned
Everyone in our village knew
They looked down upon my mother and her children
Yet, my father, Juan Duarte, was a rich man
He already had a wife and family in the Chivilcoy city area
My mother, Juana Ibarguren, was a country girlfriend from Junim
Wealthy ranchers came to the countryside for a short time
They rode grand horses as they mustered their cattle
In the evenings, they went to the bars to relax
Young girls were attracted and seduced
After the laughter and fun, things got personal
Maybe there were promises
But, soon the tears flowed as the ranchers left
Many girls found that they were pregnant
My mother was one of them
In all, she had five children by my father
So it must have been a regular relationship
When I was one year old he left and did not return
Nor did he provide an income
We were driven to live on the poor side of town
Mother kept us alive by sewing people's clothes
Of course, I could not help being illegitimate
But, other children called me names
The priests treated my mother as an outcast
In their eyes, she had sinned more than once
There was no forgiveness
Other parents did not want us to play with their children
We lived in a one-room apartment
Life was hard
As my brothers and sisters grew older they got jobs
That helped us move to a larger house

Eva Peron

Eventually, my mother took in boarders
Therefore, I learned a lot about different people
I also had the chance learn at school
My favourite lessons were singing and dancing
In 1933, I gained a part in the school play
From that day, I knew what I wanted to do
Each night, I dreamt of being an actress
Mother, however, wanted me to marry a local boy
Maybe she was keen that I avoid her situation
I viewed marriage at such a young age with horror
Therefore, at the age of 15, I went to Buenos Aires
To her credit, Mother supported me
She helped get me lodgings with friends of my father
On arrival in the city, it took my breath away
So many people rushing in all directions
Yet all around, I saw poverty and hunger
The great economic depression meant many were out of work
Survival meant that I had to take any job
But, in the evenings, I joined the theatrical groups
By 1935, I gained my professional debut at the Comedias Theater
Ironically, in the light of future developments the title was appropriate
It was called *The Perezes Misses*
It was the start I needed to give me experience
In 1936, I toured Argentina with a theater company
Also, I gained a part in a B-grade film
My dream was beginning to come true
Still only 17 years of age, life was moving fast
I was learning a lot on stage and off
Relationships came and went as I focussed on my career
One aspect was a daily radio drama series on Radio El Mundo
Being on the largest station in the land, my name became known
As a result, Radio Belgrano offered me a five year contract
How could I refuse?
It gave me the opportunity to play some famous roles
Elizabeth I of England and the last Tsarina of Russia were two of them
All part of the *Great Women of History* series of programmes
It also gave me the chance to get shares in the company
My dream was becoming a reality in more senses than one

Eva Duarte was no longer a poor girl and looked down upon
People paid me respect and looked up to me
By 1942, I had my own apartment in one of the better districts
On the other side of the Atlantic, the Second World War raged on
It all seemed a long way away
At home, we were more concerned with local issues
Naturally, I met people of influence

We decided to form a political party
It was called the Argentine Radio Syndicate; ARA for short
However, politics of a different kind were to change my life

In January 1944, an earthquake hit the town of San Juan
Up to 10,000 people were killed and many more injured
Juan Peron was the Secretary of Labour
He established an artistic festival to raise funds for the victims
As a well known entertainer, I was invited
Afterwards at the gala party, Juan Peron complimented me
It was 22nd January 1944 and the start of many conversations
About 2am the following morning we left the party together
It was the start of many nights that would spend together
He was nearly 50 years of age and I was 25
But, that did not matter to either of us
From the start, we knew it was more than a one night stand
Unmarried, we lived together
We both had what each other needed beyond the bedroom
Of course, priests, politicians and many other people disapproved
You may say that I was following in my mother's footsteps
But, I had another dream
One that I could not share with anyone other than Juan
I wanted him to be President of Argentina
In return, he helped me become President of the Actors Union
Continuing my radio career, I often mentioned Juan's work
The programme *Towards A Better Future* supported his ideas
However, his opponents arrested him and put him in jail
On my radio programme, I called on the people to help
On 15th October 1945, about 300,000 people marched
At the Casa Rosada, they chanted and demanded Juan's release
I knew that I should speak to his supporters
Standing on the balcony, I spoke from my heart
'We must act not just talk,' I said
'The time has come to stand up for freedom and release Juan'
The crowd cheered and marched on the residence of the President
Within two days, Juan was out of prison
The leaders of the unions ensured his release
They could have paralysed the country with strikes
The President signed a decree to avoid that
In celebration, Juan and I were married the day after his release
The official ceremony in church took place on December 9th 1945
Clearly, Juan had many people on his side

On my radio show, I talked mainly to women
Previously, women had been ignored in politics
On the campaign trail I spoke at political meetings
It was then that I asked people to call me Evita
I told them that Juan could help them and their families
In addition, the unions supported him
That showed when he was swept to power in the 1946 election
Suddenly, at the age of 27, I was the President's wife
As the First Lady, I took the duties very seriously
My first big tour was to the European countries
Ravaged by Germany during the war, there was much poverty
In contrast, I was entertained in royal fashion by the leaders
The Spanish Government awarded me the Cross of Isabel the Catholic
It was their highest honour for a poor girl who had become rich
Yet in Spain, I noted the children running barefoot
Walking the streets I handed 100 peseta notes to many of them
Memories of my mother and childhood swept over me
Next, I visited Italy and met the Pope
In France, I met the President
But, there was no invitation to meet the Queen of England
In Switzerland, my car was attacked
The Rainbow Tour, as it was called, came to an end
I had learned a lot about diplomacy
But my real mission lay at home
There I founded the Eva Peron Foundation
Funding came from sources like horse racing, lotteries and casinos
Union and business leaders provided money
Within a couple of years we had over 200 million dollars
We employed over 14,000 people
Many poor people benefited as I had planned
Evita City was built in 1947 to provide housing
Beyond that, we distributed thousands of shoes and cooking materials
Hospitals and schools were built by our 6000 workers
My time was taken up day and night, supervising arrangements
Yet, most important were the meetings with sick and needy
The lepers, the syphilitics, the outcasts all came to see me
Indeed, I went to find them
For I had once been an outcast

I knew what it felt like
If I only gave them hope then it was worth it
An outcast needs to know someone cares
There were not enough hours in the day
Racing from one crisis to another sapped my energy
Many days I was working over 20 hours at a stretch
Even when I tried to sleep it was difficult
Instead of the dreams I was having nightmares
So much suffering came before my eyes each day
Even my own childhood problems seem small in comparison
Some said that I was obsessed and fanatical
Juan urged me to take more time to rest

But the poor could not rest in poverty
Political action was necessary as well as charity
Women did not have the vote
With the help Juan gave, this was achieved
As a result, I created the Female Peronist Party
By 1951, it had over 500,000 members
They helped Juan be elected as President again
Over 2,000,000 people asked me to be Vice President
But I had to say no
My energy levels were falling
At a meeting, I fainted and was taken to hospital

It was the first of many such events as I lost more weight
The doctors told me that I had cancer and needed an operation
A radical hysterectomy was performed
Cervical cancer was diagnosed
The pain got worse
But, I made one major effort to be with Juan to celebrate his victory
My women and the unions had made him President
But I would not see the results
At the age of 33 I said goodbye.

Edith Piaf
1915–1963

Most of my early years were spent in a brothel
I was living with my grandmother at the time
She was in charge of the working girls
It was a chaotic time
I was born in the middle of the First World War
Many families were torn apart through death and injury
Our family was torn apart for different reasons
My parents did not want me to restrict their lives
They were young and enjoying life, and then I arrived
Whatever plans they may have had did not involve a child
Annetta, my mother, was a café singer
She came from Italy and was of North African descent
Father was a street acrobat and worked in theatres on occasions
My parents called me Édith Giovanna Gassion
Edith in commemoration of Edith Cavell
She was the English nurse war heroine, killed by the Germans
Giovanna reflected my mother's Italian family
But, there was to be no normal family life for me
Mother left, soon after I was born
The Germans had invaded France and danger lay all around
In 1916, my father, Louis, had to join the French army
Therefore, my maternal grandmother in Paris was asked to look after me
Apparently, she did not do that properly
When my father returned, on army leave, he found scabs on my body
I was in poor health, so he took me to Normandy
Aged about two, I was left in the care of his mother
The brothel that she owned was a lively house, with many visitors
At the age of three, I began to lose my eyesight
A frightening experience that stopped me from walking and running
The doctor called it 'keratisis' and I lived in a world of darkness
Like all blind people, I had to learn new skills
Staying in the house each day, rather than playing outside
That meant that I had few friends of my own age
The working girls were good to me

Edith Piaf

They prayed, to Saint Therese of Lisieux, that my sight would return
During that time, I needed all the help the girls could offer
They brought me presents and played games
That was the main way in which I learnt to speak French
However, there were times when they did not want me around
That was when a man, or group of men, came to the house
Afterwards, they would often buy me some sweets
Eventually, I understood
Even my few friends knew
As if by a miracle, after about four years, my eyesight returned
Once I could see, the working girls thought that I may see too much
Both the local priest and my grandmother felt it best if I left
Father took me with him on his acrobatic tour of villages and towns
As Papa's assistant, I took the hat round for the collections
My other job was to look after the monkey that was part of the act
It was a vagabond gypsy style of life
Via my father's travelling show, I got to know France
Much better than any classroom geography lessons
Occasionally, when father found a girlfriend, we stayed for a while
Some of the girlfriends were good to me, but others were not
During those times, I went to the local school until the relationship ended
Once again we would set out on country roads to our next street theatre
Many times, I walked without shoes
One winter's day, Papa fell ill
We had no money, so I went to the town centre
It was a market day and I sang the only song that I knew
Our national anthem - *La Marseillaise*
Dressed in a flimsy ragged skirt and cheap blouse, I sang boldly
Yes, I sang with spirit from the heart and for my father's life
People stopped and listened
Some of them had tears in their eyes
Then, they applauded and put cash and notes on the ground
It was far more money than Papa got for his acrobatics
Many people asked who I was
'My mother has left me, and Papa is ill,' I replied
In addition to money, some people gave me food and soft drinks
I was about ten years of age and it was the start of my singing career
Papa was pleased when I gave him the food and the money

Upon his recovery, he suggested that I sing before his act
It helped bring in the crowd
There was no band or accompaniment
Just me, like a bird, singing in the open air
Learning all the words was hard as I could not read well
But, I enjoyed entertaining and gained many fans
The crowds usually shouted for more
After a few years, it was time for me to move on
As a 15 year old, I wanted to do things my own way
Living with Papa was becoming restrictive
We both needed to do our own thing, although it was sad to part
He had done his best for me, but I needed to chart my own course
Times were tough on the street
The great economic depression of the 1930s had set in
Maybe things would be better for me in Paris
I had heard a lot about the Montmartre area and went there
On arrival, I took a room at the Grand Hotel de Clermont
In the 18th district, it was not as grand as it sounded
To pay the bills, I needed to earn some money quickly
Therefore, I went into the streets and began singing for my supper
Starting in the Pigalle area, I soon drew a crowd
A young girl talked to me after one of the performances
She was homeless, like me, and we became friends
Momome was her name and she did the collections while I sang
We toured the city and lived wherever we could find a shelter
We often had to sleep in the doorway of a building
Each night, I would sing and an instant audience would form
Afterwards, in the warmth and bright lights of the bars, I made friends
Louis Dupont was one of them and he made me laugh
The stories about his work, as a delivery boy, were funny
As a 17 year old Parisian, he knew his way around
One year younger than him, I fell in love
The world seemed a beautiful place
For the first time, someone of my own age really wanted me
Within a year, I gave birth to Marcelle, our daughter
As a 17 year old, I was not ready for a child
Singing on the streets and a full night life kept me happy
It did not go with motherhood

Louis was often left with the baby, while I was out working and drinking
Neither of us found our new responsibilities easy
The problems became worse, as our daughter became ill
'Meningitis,' the doctor said
There was nothing that could be done and she wasted away
When Marcelle died, at the age of two, I left Louis
That was how I came face-to-face with my previous world
My next boyfriend, Albert, was a pimp for prostitutes
We talked about my early years and my childhood in a brothel
He wanted me to be one of his working girls
I needed some protection, but not for that kind of work
Instead, we agreed he would get a commission from my street singing
In return, he would help draw the crowd and collect the money
It was a shady world and one of my friends, Nadia, killed herself
While working for Albert, he had put her under severe pressure
After that happened, I broke off my relationship with him
Being of a violent disposition, he nearly shot me when I left
On my own again, I continued singing in the Montmartre streets
It was a hand to mouth type of existence, spending everything I earned
After one evening session, a well dressed man came over
He said his name was Louis Leplée, a nightclub owner
'You sang very well,' he said, 'I would like you to do some work for me'
We went for a drink and he invited me to Le Gerny
It was an up-market club near the Champs-Elysees
On the day arranged, I slept in after an all-night drinking session
Arriving one hour late for the appointment, I was a little out of breath
It was an up-market club near the Champs-Elysées
He immediately asked me to sing to people in the club
Surprisingly, I was nervous performing on a proper stage
Being small, for I was only 147 centimetres in height, did not help
My clothes needed upgrading and my hairstyle had to be improved
Louis Leplée was helpful and told me to wear a black dress
It became my trademark
He also called me *La Môme Piaf*, the little sparrow
Louis also taught me how to perform on stage
Then, he organised a big concert and asked me to be the lead singer
Many famous people came, including Maurice Chevalier
After that, I gained a recording contract and made two albums

At the club, I met Jacques Borgeat, a poet who became a good friend
I believed in him, as he helped me write and learn about literature
In contrast, Louis Leplée, was a different kind of believer
I felt safe with him, as I realised he was gay and a loner
Louis believed that I could be a big star on stage and radio
'You need a memorable stage name,' he said one evening
'Édith Giovanna Gassion is too long and too foreign'
On the street and in the music halls, I had many stage names
Tania, Denise, and Jay were just some of them
None of those names appealed to Louis

We agreed to use my first name with a name he gave me
He called me 'Piaf', the street name for a little sparrow
So, that is how, in 1935 at the age of 20, I became Edith Piaf
Easy to remember, hard to forget
Often, I was referred to as 'Kid Piaf', being so small
Louis helped me earn more money than I had ever seen
Most of it was spent entertaining my friends in the Pigalle bars

That was where I felt most at home, amongst the laughter and drinks
It was a shock when, in 1936, Louis Leplée was murdered
The police thought that I was involved and so did some of the press
The mobsters who killed him were part of my past
Theatre audiences turned against me because of the affair
Again, I needed protection and turned to Raymond Asso
An ex-French Legionnaire, born in Morocco, he was tough
In Paris, he had many contacts and was a nightclub manager
We met because he was writing songs
He wrote some for me and we soon became lovers
However, to gain a wider audience, I toured the provinces
It helped me escape the pressures of Paris and the innuendo
Following the tours, my singing and acting careers took off
From the late 1930s, my stage name was in lights
Le Bel Indifferent, a play, with Jean Cocteau, in 1940, was successful
However, the sound of guns filled the air around Paris
France fell once again under the jackboots of the Nazi Army
The Second World War had begun war and the capital was invaded
The German occupation of our country disrupted *la belle vie*
Raymond was conscripted into the armed forces
The German invasion wrecked our lives
I needed friends, not enemies
Paul Meurisse became my new lover, as I could not bear living alone
Also, Momone returned
Andree Bigard became my manager and helped me a lot
She organised shows for the French prisoners in the German Stalag III
On occasions, some of them escaped, disguised as orchestra members
That was most exciting and a cause for long celebrations
Indeed, my lifestyle revolved around drinking, singing and sleeping
For two years during the war, I lived, once again, in a brothel
Though I did not need that kind of work to survive
The people and the shows helped keep me sane during the dark days
Parisians needed entertainment and music to raise their spirits
So many looked to me to do that and keep their hopes alive
A French voice they could cheer above the German propaganda
Marguerite Monnot became my friend and songwriter
We composed many hit songs
Also, I discovered Yves Montand and he joined me on stage

For a while, he was the new man in my life
Many of the shows were for soldiers during the war
From 1940 to 1945, it was a time of danger
Be a *collaborateur* or be a member of the *resistance*
Those were our choices
Being well known, I was watched, but only arrested once
Even though one of my lovers, a pianist, was a Jewish guy
One of my songs, with Marguerite Monnot, was a subtle protest
We all celebrated long and hard in August 1944, when France was liberated
After the war, I went on tour with Charles Aznavour
La Vie en Rose, written in 1945, became a popular song
It was one of many that I sang on my visit to America
Other popular songs were *Hymne a L'Amour* and *Les Trois Cloches*
Milord and *Mon Legionnaire* were also well received
My shows at the Versailles, New York, sold out
Likewise, when I returned to Europe there were many big shows
During that time, I met Marcel Cerdan, from Algeria
He was the middleweight world boxing champion
A man who I believed would love and protect me
Although he was married, we had a whirlwind romance
After his divorce, we wed, but disaster struck
An Air France flight crashed, killing him and everyone on board
My world had been shattered once again
More problems followed in 1951
A car crash, when driving with Charles Aznavour, left me with injuries
Breaking both arms and ribs, I was given pain killers
Two other car crashes left me in more pain
It led to a serious morphine addiction
Also, my need for alcohol caused other complications
In search of love, I married Jacques Pills in 1952
It was an up-and-down emotional roller coaster of a life
Four years later we divorced
Singing kept me sane during all the problems
It was important not to let my fans down
Each year from 1955 to 1962, I appeared at Paris Olympia
It was a time when more men came into and out of my life
Hope invariably turned to disappointment
Was I in search of the perfect man?

One thing was for sure, I wanted a perfect song
One that defined me and one that I could make my own
In 1960, two songwriters, Charles Daumont and Michel Vaucaire visited me
Would this one be any different from the hundreds that I had rejected?
'What is the title of your song?' I asked them directly
Michel just handed me the lyrics
'Non, je ne regrette rien'

I stopped and read the title once again
'Non, je ne regrette rien'
No, I do not regret anything
Those few words summed up my philosophy and my life
Take the risks and live with the consequences
'Ask for forgiveness, but never permission'
Those were my sentiments

At the time, I was 45 years of age
I asked Charles to play the music on the piano
Immediately, I knew the song was written for me personally
Of all the music I recorded, that song made my name famous
Not just in France, but worldwide
It was first performed at Olympia, Paris, in 1961
The audience was entranced and then rose to applaud
One of many performances that would always bring people to their feet
But, I was still in search of a man who would sweep me off my feet
The next year, I married again
Theo Sarapo was an actor and singer, twenty years younger than me
He was openly gay and people questioned my judgement
Not for the first time
No doubt, he questioned his own judgement with what was to come
For a long time, my pains had been getting worse
Medication did not work
Nor did the drink and non-prescribed drugs
'What is causing the pain?' I asked the doctor
'Liver cancer,' he replied
There was no cure
In addition, my debts were mounting and the income was declining
Fame remained, but not the fortune
In October 1963, although only 48 years old, I said goodbye
It was a simple message
Je ne regrette rien.

Maria Poliakova
1910–(c)1990

The secret messages from Germany began in September 1942
They were messages that could save millions of lives
Each message gave specific details
Outlining the incredible plans being developed by the Nazis
Our spy network in Switzerland were amazed
The listening post was in touch with 'Werther'
A spy at Hitler's table
Someone at the heart of the Nazi Government
Someone who knew where the German Military would attack next
The messages indicated the specific targets to be attacked
Cities and towns across the 1,800 miles of Russian borders were named
Could the messages be relied upon, or were they a trap?
It was vital to know
Stalin, our leader, was told and he ignored the information
He said it was a German plan to mislead him and our troops
On June 22nd 1941, Hitler had given the order to invade Russia
Millions of our people were being killed and wounded
Soldiers on the battlefields were annihilated
Civilians in our cities and towns were bombed
Prisoners were shot, or put in concentration camps
The Second World War was devastating all the countries of Europe
Could the secret messages help stop the carnage?
The messages kept arriving on our receiver in Switzerland
It was my job to co-ordinate the work at our spy post
I had been trained by the master spies of the Soviet Union
As a young fervent communist in Russia, my talent was noticed
I was fluent in various languages
French, German, English and Russian were the main ones
It gave me the ability to understand secrets in many languages
As a young girl, I had travelled to Germany, France and Switzerland
My father was a senior official with the Soviet Trade Commissariat
We lived wherever he worked
My ambition was to become a doctor
That changed when I met Jan Karlovich Berzin

Maria Poliakova

He was Head of the Red Army Intelligence
At the age of 24, he recruited me to be a 'fighter' for our country
He said that my Government needed me to work as a spy in Germany
It was a difficult decision
As an unmarried mother, I had to leave my child behind
For the good of our communist cause, I packed my bags in 1934
Hitler had come to power the previous year and Nazism was on the rise
My orders were top secret
They involved making friends
Not social friends, but communist friends who supported the cause
It took me a year to find people that I could trust
Then, the training started and my friends were sworn to secrecy
On my return to Moscow, I gave a detailed report
After more intensive training, I was sent to Switzerland in 1936
Such a beautiful country
But, there was no time to see the sights
I was the co-ordinator for Soviet spies in Europe
Crossing the border, I visited my friends in Germany
Also, I formed a spy ring in Switzerland
My contacts were known as 'Gisela's family'
Other members were Sonia, Sissy, Gilbert, Jim, Le Grand Chef and Lucy
Most important of all was Werther, who was lying low in Germany
By 1937, political problems at home meant that I had to return to Russia
Stalin was widening his purges
Berzin, my mentor, had been killed
Would I be accused?
In the Kremlin, I was given menial work
My network of spies were ignored
Then, days of sadness when I heard my father and brothers were dead
They were declared enemies of the Russian people and shot
Ironically, Stalin did not put me on the list
In Switzerland, the spy network, I had developed, was dormant
So were Werther and my friends in Germany
There could be a time when they were needed
The Second World War was declared in 1939
However, it was 1940 before real action took place
Hitler had signed a pact with Stalin
It was a mutual non-aggression agreement

Ribbentrop from Germany and Molotov from the Soviet Union signed it
It seemed that my spies might not be needed
But neither Hitler nor Stalin believed the pact would last
Nazism and Communism could not co-exist
My friends in Germany said it was only a matter of time
The Nazi military attack would come soon
I reported this, but Stalin ignored the messages
He also ignored warnings from many others

My friends in Germany were correct
On June 22nd 1941, Hitler's Nazis invaded Russia without warning
Our Soviet troops were not prepared and suffered great losses
The Germans killed and maimed all in their path
Our communist homeland was being reduced to ruins
Where would the Nazis strike next?
We needed information on the their plans
It was time to ask my friends in Germany for help

Of course, it took time for them to make arrangements
During this period, our troops defended heroically
Especially at Stalingrad
From July 17th 1942 till February 2nd 1943 they fought and won
In the middle of this gigantic battle, my friends made a breakthrough
Martin Bormann was the second-in-command to Hitler
He persuaded him to have stenographers at meetings
To record the so-called greatness of his speeches and decisions
Hitler liked that
Being vain, he wanted the world to know of his achievements
Bormann selected the stenographers himself
One of my friends was appointed
It meant access to the highest level of Nazi decision-making
At last, we had a chance of finding out the secret plans
Our spy was at OKQ, the high command of the German forces
Shortly afterwards, the coded messages began to arrive in Switzerland
My friend Werther was giving us priceless secrets
I had provided Werther with a transmitter and wireless frequency
The information came to our listening post day after day
Places, names, battle plans
Military secrets of the top order
All the information was sent to the Kremlin
Stalin was suspicious
He was always suspicious
Initially, he ignored the secrets, suspecting a deception
More towns and cities were lost to the Germans
The secret messages continued to flow in
Eventually, the accuracy of the information convinced Stalin
Werther was a gold mine of secret military intelligence
Surely it could not last
There must have been suspicions in Germany
If so, then no one told Hitler
His table talk continued to be broadcast to Switzerland
There, my network decoded and passed on the valuable secrets
But, the Swiss were closing in on our group
They did not want their neutrality disturbed by a scandal
We had to close the listening station
Our spy group dispersed

I returned to Russia
The spy machine was not found until after the war
When they did locate it, there were many messages on the printer
Werther had continued to operate, even though we could not do so
A brave friend and extra special spy.

Irena Sendler
1910–2008

Scared, I walked towards the exit of the ghetto
Two big German guards were checking people's papers
Would I be inspected and caught?
Inside my medical case was an infant
Her parents had died the previous week
There was no future for the child in the ghetto
That is why I decided to smuggle her out in my case
What if the baby cried as I queued at the exit?
As I walked to the gate, each minute seemed like an hour
Was I doing the right thing for the baby?
Would I be searched?
The Germans had captured the Jews of Warsaw
I was one of the few people allowed into the ghetto
My job was to try and limit the spread of disease
The conditions under which people lived were appalling
Typhus and other diseases were spreading
As a trained nurse, I treated as many as possible
The Germans did not care how many people died
They were sending the Jews to the 'death camps' anyway
Contagious diseases, however, could kill their own men
To reduce the risk, they allowed me into the ghetto
It was then that I realised more needed to be done
Particularly, to save Jewish children
My parents had always done their best to help people
That is what they would want me to do
I was born in a small town, Otwock, in Poland
Later, we moved to Tarczyn
It was the time of the First World War
My father was Dr Krzyżanowska, a small-town doctor
I noted that many of his patients were Jewish people
He and my mother brought me up to respect them
As a young girl, I got to know a number of the patients
Mothers brought their children to his surgery and we played
Sadly, in 1917, my father died during a typhus epidemic

Irena Sendler

After that, the Jewish people stopped coming to our house
However, I remembered my friends
Sometimes, we would meet in the street and play
As I grew older, I noticed that they had different ways
They went to church on a Saturday
We went to the Catholic Church on a Sunday
Eventually, I understood the differences
Old Testament, New Testament
Abraham and Christ, both Jews
Poland was a home for many of them
Their children were born there, just as I was
They were as Polish as me
Life for them and for me became harder
The Nazi Party, led by Hitler, was elected in Germany
From 1933, our country was under threat
Hitler said he would take our land and kill people
Racist policies were introduced
I was 23 years old at the time
My studies for a career as a social worker had just started
Each day, I witnessed the problems faced by the Jews
There was an anti-Jewish element in work and education
One third of the students at one time were Jews
Hitler's speeches stirred up more racial conflict, also in Poland
Opposing such action, I made my views known at Warsaw University
The officials barred me from being a student for three years
In 1935, at Lwow Polytechnic, the Jewish students were segregated
Ghetto benches meant Jews had to sit together
It was a sign of things to come
In due course, I gained a job at the Social Welfare Department
Some of us realised what would happen if war started
We tried to help Jews who wanted to leave
Over 3,000 false documents were created to facilitate this
By 1939, Poland was invaded by the Germans
Poles fought bravely, but were killed without mercy
The days of Nazi rule and the holocaust had begun
Within days, the racist regulations were posted
On October 16th, the Warsaw Ghetto was established
In an area of about 16 blocks, over 450,000 people were imprisoned

Disease soon became rife, particularly typhus
It is estimated that more than 100,000 died
But, the ghetto was only a staging post for the real death camps
Treblinka was one of many
About 300,000 people from the ghetto were sent there to be gassed
At the time, it was called deportation
But, we could guess the real purpose
What could be done to help the families?

'Zegota' was a codename for an underground organisation
Its purpose was to find places of safety for Jewish people
It was organised by both Jews and non-Jews
I joined and was put in charge of the children's section
Everything had to be done in secret
To be caught meant Nazi torture and almost certain death
Therefore, I was given the codename 'Jolanta'
Brave people, like my colleague Irena Schultz, helped me
My full-time job was with the Government Welfare Department

Therefore, I had a German 'special permit' to enter the ghetto
Officially, my job was to report on conditions and control disease
Needless to say, the job was dangerous in more senses than one
On my visits, I witnessed many horrors
Living conditions were abominable
People's bones showed through, as there was little food
Sanitation became worse with so many people in the ghetto
Yet, the Jews tried to keep things organised
They had soup kitchens, schools and secret religious services
The Jews were required to wear the Star of David by the Germans
I did it to show I was not a German and there to help
It was impossible to secure the safety of adults
However, could I help some children?
Consulting with some trusted colleagues, I developed a plan
Why not smuggle some of them out of the ghetto?
Of course, there were many risks
Not least was that the Jewish parents were suspicious
Where would the children go and would they be safe?
In truth, I did not know, as there were no guarantees
But, one thing I was sure about
If the children stayed in the ghetto, they would die
Some Jewish parents understood that, some did not
That is why I decided to smuggle an orphan
The baby was only a few weeks old
At the exit, there was a long queue of working men
Should I wait in line, or take a risk?
It was unusual for a woman to have a permit into the ghetto
Would a German officer search an Aryan woman?
I could not afford to wait in line
Waving my nurse's badge, I kept walking
None of the Polish workers said anything
At the gate, I showed my papers to a German officer
He examined it and asked what was in my case
'Samples of diseased material for laboratory analysis,' I said
Hoping that he would avoid putting himself at risk of infection
Inside the Jewish infant slept with the aid of a sedative
After what seemed an age, he waved his hand
The gate opened and I walked into the city

It was as if I was walking on air
My first call was to the Sisters of the Family of Mary
The Mother Superior asked no questions
I had found an orphan
It did not matter if it was a Catholic or Jewish child
So many parents were dead or dying
The child needed the protection of the Church
We said a prayer, as I handed the baby to her
In my other hand, I had the name of the child
On returning home, I put the name in a jar
When it was dark, I went into my garden
The jar was buried beneath an apple tree
Better to bury the name, not the child
It was the first of many names that would go in the jar
In the following weeks, and months, I continued
Inside the ghetto, families heard what I was doing
The first time a mother gave her baby to me it was dreadful
'Will our child be safe?' the father asked anxiously
'If the child stays in the ghetto, it will certainly die,' I said
Both parents were in tears and so was I
Promising to return with news, I left with their baby
On my next visit, they had tears of joy
Their baby had been adopted by a Protestant family
On other visits, some parents came to me with their children
Would I take them to relatives?
Some of the children were five years old and more
How could I smuggle a child of that size?
New ways had to be found
For babies, I used suitcases and boxes
Some brave workmen put the babies in their tool kit
For older children, I had to smuggle them in ambulances
Some were genuinely sick, others were made to look ill
Each time, I took their name and put it in the jar
It listed where they had been placed
Convents were helpful, especially one of them
The Little Sister Servants of the Blessed Virgin Mary
Located at Turkowide and Chotomow near Warsaw
Parish priests also helped

Families of those in the ghetto were at risk
However, their non-Jewish friends took in children
No one refused to have a child, despite the war problems
Of course, the children had to lose their Jewish identity
The risks became greater when I involved others
As things got worse, the number of babies offered increased

Their parents knew that death was only a matter of time
They agreed it was better for their children to be fostered
Often, I lay awake at night wondering what to do
The issue was becoming more urgent
The deportations to the death camps were increasing

'Operation Reinhard' had started in July 1942
It was soon a well-organised system
Cattle train wagons full of Jews left for the gas chambers
Treblinka and other death camps were the destinations
My team of collaborators increased their efforts
Many new ways of smuggling had to be invented
Small babies were strapped to a stretcher with a sick adult
It was hoped the guards would not look under the blanket
Older children escaped through small tunnels
The old courthouse, next to the ghetto, was used
Many children escaped through the dank, dark, smelly sewers
Some were carried in potato bags
Even coffins and body bags were used
The ingenuity to cheat the Germans of another killing was incredible
It is hard to be sure how many children escaped
It is estimated that between 2,500 and 3,000 were smuggled out
On escaping the ghetto, they were still hunted by the Germans
The Nazis were determined to kill every Jew they could find
They were also killing those who assisted them
I realised that the next arranged escape could be my last one
Inevitably, the Nazis would discover what I was doing
In 1943, they arrested me and took me to a place of torture
Pawiak Prison
For hours and hours, they demanded that I give them names
I refused, so they beat me, breaking my bones
They wanted the names of people who had helped me
'Tell us the names of your conspirators,' they shouted
I closed my eyes and said nothing
'You will tell us all of the names,' they shrieked, as they got more angry
Of course, they wanted the names of the children
Names of those who had slipped through their murdering hands
Next they came with a list
'We demand the names of the foster parents,' screamed an officer
'Names of the priests'
'Names of the nuns'
'You will give us their names or you will die,' he concluded
When I did not, they broke my arms
'Names, names, names,' they shouted in anger

Then they broke my legs
'You will give us the names,' they screamed
When I recovered consciousness a Nazi officer was there
'This is your last chance to give us the names and save your life,'
When I refused to answer, they condemned me to death
That, I thought, would be the end of it
Just before I was due to be shot, a German officer was bribed
My friends found the money to do a deal
En route to the place of death, I was left unconscious in a forest
My friends found me
When I regained consciousness, I was very scared
Would the Germans find me again for more torture?
My friends said the Nazis were not looking for me
'Why?' I asked
'The Germans have officially listed you as dead,' replied my friend
My name was on a public notice board of those executed
Gradually, with good care, my bones healed
The war raged on, with more terror in the streets
Not least from the Russians who drove out the Germans in 1945
It was the Germans' turn to be deported on trains
After the war, I returned to my garden and started digging
There, I found the jars with the names of the children
How many were still alive?
It became my mission to find out
However, I had other problems
Following the stress of war, my marriage was dissolved
That was a difficult time but I did not feel alone
Out there, I knew there were children I had saved
In due course, I met Stefan Zgrzembski
It took time for me to tell him about the ghetto
He was kind and understood
He then realised that I had a wider family
The task was to find them and give them their family names
It was a major task
However, it was interrupted by another attack
After the war, Poland was controlled by Communist Russia
They accused me of links to the Polish Government in Exile
More dark days in prison, as I was arrested again

This time the torture was more psychological than physical
More names were demanded
Names of my colleagues, friends and associates
Eventually, I was let out of prison and continued my work
The only names that mattered to me were in the jar
The names of the children we had smuggled to safety
Could we find the parents of the children on the lists?
Of course, most had been killed in the Nazi gas chambers
There were sad days when we had to tell the children
But, we did have a few successes
On those occasions, there were great celebrations
In due course, I celebrated by becoming a mother
Fortunately, I had three children of my own
However, one died as an infant
Our other children grew up healthy, but with discrimination
We explained to our son and daughter the issues
'Because of my work, you could have difficulties,' I said
Indeed they did
Both were denied the right to study at university
The hatred in my own country still continued
It did not stop me trying to find the parents of the children
But, my Jewish friends showed their appreciation
In 1965, they recognised me with a Yad Vashem medal
The Righteous Among the Nations Award
Also, they awarded me the Commander's Cross of the Israeli Institute
However, it was not until 2003 that Poland recognised my work
The Order of the White Cross was awarded
Sixty years after the Jewish children were rescued from the ghetto
In 2007, Poland's Senate nominated me for the Nobel Peace Prize
Elzbieta Ficowska, who I had rescued, conveyed appreciation
She represented all of the children we helped to escape
Every one of them was part of my family
Other children from the USA and elsewhere came to see me
I told them, 'You cannot separate people by race or religion'
'You can only separate people by good and evil'
'The good will always triumph.'

Kato Shizue
1897–2001

At the age of 17, I was married
My parents felt that they had done the right thing
The marriage was arranged, not one of free choice
Baron Ishimoto Keikichi was much older than me
He was wealthy and well-connected
Tradition in Japan was very strong
The roles for men and women had long been defined
Men were expected to be the bread winners
Women were expected to look after the family and home
I was born into a rich Japanese family that respected tradition
Therefore, my parents expected me to do likewise
Nevertheless, they had a wider view than most
Father visited western countries on business
My mother was well educated and read Shakespeare
Despite this, mother said, 'a man comes first, a woman follows'
Instead of being free to choose, I took on my role as a wife
It meant following my husband to places that I did not like
He worked as an engineer for the Mitsui organisation
We moved to live in a coal mining community
Located at Miike, Kyushu, it was a depressing world for me
Each day, everyone faced the dust, dirt and poor living conditions
It was hard for the men, and also hard for the women
They struggled to bring up their families with few facilities
While living in the community, I had two children
After three years, I was pleased to leave
The experience, however, weighed on my mind
Other women could not escape
My husband's new job was in America
In 1919, we boarded a ship and sailed across the Pacific Ocean
A journey to a new world, so different from the coal mines
In New York, I studied English and did a secretarial course
The attitudes and culture were more liberal than in Japan
However, in one regard the two places were very similar
There was little or no discussion about women's health

Kato Shizue

The subject of birth control was swept under the carpet
Margaret Sanger was the exception
She spoke out for women's rights, but was attacked
We became friends and I invited her to Japan
Initially, she was refused a visa by the Japanese Government
Eventually, in 1922, they agreed her entry on one condition
Margaret was not to give birth control lectures in public
Despite political opposition, she spoke to various groups
We met in people's homes and discussed women's health issues
That was her message, but few men understood it
Politicians and business leaders held the positions of power
They expected women to keep quiet and follow their leadership
Women's health was not on their agenda
Birth control was regarded as a taboo subject
To educate people, it was necessary to start a new organisation
As a result, The Japan Birth Control Study Group was formed
Of course, there was much disdain and opposition from men
Except Kato Kanju, a miners' leader
He asked me to speak to the wives of his members
In 1923, I began the first of my women's health lecture tours
My activities were severely frowned upon by the Government
Later, we formed a research unit and published *Small Family*
It provided useful information for women
When I opened a woollen yarn shop to sell clothes
Everyone knew I was really giving advice on birth control
The Great Kanto Earthquake of 1923 destroyed my shop
Fortunate to survive, I helped in the reconstruction work
At the same time, I was helping represent women
In truth, they did not have many political rights
They were dependent on their families and their husbands
In my case, I followed my husband again
For six months, we went on a business project to London,
My children remained with family members in Tokyo
It was a great strain being away from them for so long
On my return, I continued my work with women
However, my marriage was beginning to decline
No longer prepared to follow, I decided to focus on my work
In addition, my two sons needed more of my time

However, my reputation was becoming stronger in the USA
In 1932, I was invited to visit and talk to women about our work
I wrote a book, *Facing Two Ways*, in 1935
It was a bestseller in the USA
With the money from both activities, clinics were opened in Japan
However, politicians saw me as a troublemaker
The Government closed my clinics, saying they were outside the law

By going to the USA in 1937 to lecture, I further upset key opponents
The right-wing Japanese Government put me on a list of 'subversives'
Secret government agents, the 'thought police' contacted the civil police
On my return, on December 15th 1937, I was arrested
The charge stated that I was promoting dangerous thoughts
Two weeks in prison, during a cold December, were a warning
Next, they raided my Birth Control Consultation Clinic

That meant our work, in effect, ceased until after the Second World War
During the war, one of my sons died of tuberculosis
By 1944, my husband and I had divorced
One of the reasons was that I was in love with Kanju Kato
The union leader who had supported my work in the early days
We married in 1944, when I was 47 and he was 52
I thought there was no need for birth control in my own case
Ironically, the next year I found I was pregnant

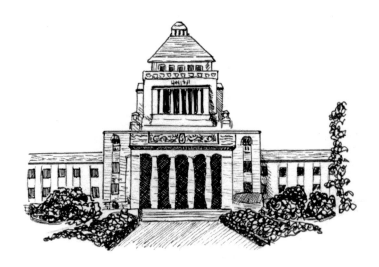

The Diet Building

My daughter was born in 1945, bringing me great happiness
But, it was also a time of despair
Japan had been beaten in the war and destroyed
There was chaos all around
Atom bombs on Hiroshima and Nagasaki were the *coup de grace*
Rebuilding Japan required new ideas
It needed new people to plan and give hope
Therefore, I decided to be a candidate for our new political Diet
The people elected me to be the first woman on the ruling body

It was yet another new challenge
One in which I was required to lead not follow
My focus was on women's rights
In particular, enabling the sale of contraceptives
Beyond this, I fought for a family planning system
Eugenic Protection Consultation Centres were established
Margaret Sanger, my mentor from the USA, visited again
Her visit created many news stories in the press to support the cause
The Family Planning Federation of Japan was formed in 1954
We were organised and funded with the support of Government
In 1955, I helped organise a major meeting in Tokyo
The International Conference on Planned Parenthood
A major advance from the small beginnings
The real results were for the benefit of women
Infant mortality and maternal deaths decreased rapidly
Doctors, instead of ignoring us, began consulting with us
The politicians also recognised our work
Government policy started to address the needs and rights of women
Maybe it was just self-interest, reflecting a wider problem
The Government saw the danger of overpopulation
Japan, an island nation, needed to feed its people
To do so, control of the population was essential
We now had major support for our work
Yet, there was still much to do and I continued my efforts
Seeing the emergence of a new Japanese woman
A well-educated generation of young articulate women
With new leaders, working for women's health and rights
Therefore, in 1974, it was time for me to move on
Having served in the parliament of Japan for over 25 years
Although for me it was time to retire, a torch had been lit
One that would continue to burn brightly
Fortunately, I lived until I was 104 and saw many changes.

Sojourner Truth
1797–1883

Born into slavery, I was sold many times
The first time it happened, I was only eight years old
It was a frightening experience
I tried to hide, but they found me
Mother cried and shouted, but it made no difference
Slaves were sold and bought by white folk
We were just a commodity like a machine or a house
It was a business deal and human feelings did not count
My parents had 13 children
They worked for Colonel Hardenbergh
He had an estate about 100 miles north of New York City
At birth, my given names were Isabella Baumfree
From a young age, I worked in the fields
It was a Dutch speaking area and that was the only language I knew
On the day I was sold, I heard the men talking
I was traded for a flock of sheep and about 100 dollars
My new master, John Neely was a hard man and I suffered badly
He seemed to enjoy beating his slaves
The mental cruelty was even worse
I had no family to talk to or to protect me
In 1808, aged 11, I was sold to Martinus Schryver for 105 dollars
He owned a tavern and I worked long hours
In the process, I learned a lot about cleaning and cooking
That lasted for about 18 months
In 1810, I was told to pack my clothes
My new owner was John Dumont of West Park, New York
At the age of 13, I went to work on his estate
The price agreed was 175 dollars as I was stronger
Most importantly, the new owner hoped I would have children
Various suggestions were made to me
However, I wanted to make my own choice
In 1815, I fell in love with a boy called Robert
He was owned by another slave master called Mr Catlin
He was a harsh man with a temper

Sojourner Truth

When he knew of our relationship he became very angry
He forbade Robert to see me and beat him
He knew that any children I had would be owned by my master
But I was already pregnant with Robert's child
Sadly, I never saw Robert again, although I thought of him often
Our daughter Diana was born in 1815
Once again the mental cruelty hit me every day for weeks
My master wanted me to have more children
Therefore, Dumont married me off to an older slave that he owned
That was how it was
No choice
Soon, I was pregnant again and worried
How would I look after another child?
Would it survive?
If my child lived, what sort of a life would it have?
Could I cope if my children were taken from me and sold?
As the years rolled by I did my duty
What option did I have?
The five children I had became Dumont's property
Peter was born in 1821 and Elizabeth in 1825
Sophia was born the next year
My other child, Thomas, tragically died soon after birth
In between having children, I worked hard
Aged nearly 30, I was healthy but unhappy
There seemed no future for me but slavery
Then, one day I heard that the law was going to change
The whisper was that slavery would be abolished
It seemed like a dream
So, I asked Mr Dumont
Apparently, New York State had been discussing it since 1791
He told me he would free me before the new law was passed
Then, he changed his mind
I was furiously angry
Also, he sold my son Peter who was only five years of age
What happened to my mother was happening to me
Therefore, I made a plan
After all, I have been working for slave masters for 20 years
One night, I picked up my daughter Sophia and left

I did not run off, for I thought that wicked
Instead, I walked off openly and with dignity
It was not an easy thing to do
My other children I had to leave behind
We all cried many tears as I set off into the night
It was a tiring journey over rough roads
Eventually, I stopped at a house owned by white folk
Isaac and Maria Van Wagener gave me work and shelter
They were people who attended church
By offering me a bed they showed Christian charity
It was the first that I had ever experienced
With their help, I commenced a legal case
My son, Peter, had been sold illegally by Dumont
Therefore, I lodged a case and won
It proved that white men's laws could be used by black folk
To my knowledge, it was first time a slave had won a legal case
The result was that I was able to regain my son
Also, on July 4th 1827 the New York emancipation law was passed
That gave me and others a new chance
What could I do with my freedom?
In 1829, we moved to New York City
It was a time to start again as a free person
In doing so, I became a devout Christian
It was the start of my campaign for equality for all
Prejudice was still there each day on the streets
For years, I worked hard for equal rights
My work with Robert Matthews brought controversy
He was a firebrand evangelist and I was his housekeeper
When another evangelist died we were accused
Fortunately, justice once again prevailed and I was acquitted
My work for the church continued
I became a Methodist and travelled widely to preach
This involved joining a group supporting women's right
We lived on a country property but could not support ourselves
So, I went to work for Mr Benson
Instead of being a slave, I was paid a wage
In 1843, I decided to change my name
That is how I became Sojourner Truth

Indeed, the truth about slavery had to be proclaimed
The country was about to enter a new era
My task was to encourage and inspire others
Therefore, I made many speeches
One of them caught the public's imagination in Akron

My speech was to the Ohio Women's Rights Convention
It was called *Ain't I A Woman?*
It was one of many times that I spoke out
I also worked on the *Ohio Anti Slavery Bugle*
A home had been bought with the money I earned

In 1857, I sold it and moved to Harmonia, Michigan
Yet, there was no harmony in our nation
The southern states were still slave states
They wanted to secede from the nation
So the Union and Confederate forces fought toe to toe
It was a fight for civil rights for people like me
I helped recruit African American troops for the Union Army
Freedom from slavery was at stake
Therefore, I worked day and night for the cause
In Washington, I worked at the Freedman's Hospital
It was a place were elderly black people got some care
On my days off, I rode in streetcars to force desegregation
That caused trouble, but it was worth it
Action rather than talk was required
The abolition of slavery did not mean equal rights
Therefore, I continued my work
In 1870, I tried to get land rights for black people
Of course, the white people still had the land
They did not want to give it to ex-slaves
Gradually, reforms were achieved and black men got the vote
Women, however, both black and white, did not have it
My campaigns continued including one against capital punishment
However, my energies were waning
In my life, I had seen many changes
Having started as the daughter of slave, I was a slave
Walking to freedom was the best thing I did
I was not given freedom
I took it
From that day, I tried to make the best use of it
May everyone who is born free respect it
May those who are still not free fight for it
That is a natural human right.

Harriet Tubman
1820-1913

I was 29 years of age when I made my first escape
That is a long time to live under a slave system
My parents were slaves for the Brodess family
Working on their land in Dorchester, Maryland
We were just one of many slave families in the area
I was the fifth of my mother's nine children
She named me Araminta 'Minty' Ross
It was not long before I knew what slavery meant
Childhood games soon came to an end
As soon as possible, I was forced to work
Rented out at the age of six to help with weaving
The owners took away my childhood
My existence was controlled by them
They could beat me when they wanted
They had no regard for us as individuals
In their eyes, slaves were like machines to do their bidding
If we did not, then we were whipped
Taking ill with measles, I was sent back to Mr Brodess
When I recovered, he rented me out to someone else
On one occasion I was accused of stealing some sugar
To avoid punishment, I hid in a pig sty
For five days, I managed to avoid capture
Hunger eventually drove me back to the slave owner's house
No one wanted to listen to my view of events
The owner was judge, jury and master of the punishment
Like cattle, we were treated as their property
If they wanted, they could sell any one of us
Three of my sisters were sold
My mother grieved, as her family was broken apart
Eventually, she took a stand
When they tried to sell one of my brothers, she stood in the way
She was so angry that the slave owner backed off
At the age of 11, I was declared an adult for work purposes
That was the age when I took my mother's name of Harriet

Harriet Tubman

About this time, I was involved in a serious incident
A metal bolt was thrown at another slave
Being nearby, it hit me on the head
As a result, I had headaches and dizzy spells
These continued throughout my life
Every day was hard work, except Sunday
If the slave owner was religious, we went to church
For the other six days, in all weather, we worked outside
It meant working in the fields before I was a teenager
The other task for female slaves was to have children
The owners wanted the next generation of slaves
It saved them having to buy new ones
A number of boys approached me
Like me, they were slaves
I wanted someone who could offer a better future
At the age of 20, I married John Tubman
He was much older than me and a free man
On reflection, was my marriage for convenience or love?
Maybe it was both
I hoped marriage would enable me to gain my freedom
'Manumitted' was the term they gave to freed slaves
They had usually been a slave for a long time
The owner could therefore reward them with freedom
But, where could the former slave go?
If they left, they could be seized and put into slavery again
Anyone of a dark colour skin was assumed to be a slave
There was little point in walking into town proclaiming freedom
However, I thought that John could help me become free
It was not to be and I continued as a slave
Even if I was free, what else could I do?
In my case, I was illiterate
Slaves were deliberately kept away from education
What work could we do without an education?
But I had a good memory and could solve problems
I could also dream about freedom
They could not stop me doing that
Many nights I fell asleep planning my escape
Could my dreams become reality?

Or would they become a nightmare?
By the age of 29, I had enough courage to try
Also, my marriage was falling apart
Another reason for getting away
The prospect of another year of slavery appalled me
Soon, I would be too old and weak
To escape, it was necessary to be strong and healthy
Two of my brothers agreed to come with me
Trying to cross the Mason–Dixon line
Our intention was to get to Philadelphia
Slavery had been abolished there
Therefore, we set off on a weekend
Our absence would not be noticed till the Monday
We made good progress northwards
Then, we heard a ransom was on our heads
We feared for our family
Therefore, with heavy hearts, we returned
Punishment was expected and delivered
But, it did not deter me
My dream of escaping was still with me
Then, the situation changed
Mr Brodess, the slave owner, died
His wife decided to sell some slaves
At the time, I had been ill
As I was unable to work, she put my name on the list
That was the day that I made up my mind
When I recovered from the illness, I established a plan
Liberty or death!
The second time, I would escape alone
In 1849, I set off
No one to rely on, except myself
The previous trial run proved useful, as I knew the way
Keeping to the back roads and travelling at night
En route, I met some Quakers who helped
They gave me food and shelter and guidance
When I crossed the border, I gave a shout of joy
However, new problems were just beginning
It was necessary to find some work to pay my way

That was not easy, as I only had basic farming skills
On getting a job, I felt independent for the first time
Before long, I was dreaming again
Could I establish a route to free other slaves?
Could I be a secret agent who helped them?
There was only one way to find out
That is why I returned to Maryland
My heart was beating at a fast rate
The return journey was long and lonely
The risks were high

The penalties for being caught were severe
It was like returning to the lions' den
There was danger all around
Nevertheless, it was necessary to take action
It was the only way my people could gain freedom
Within a short time, I met some slaves
We met after dark
'I know the route, if you want to escape,' I said
After a few questions, they agreed
Secretly preparing them was difficult

Loose talk would mean whippings and worse
It was the first of many hazardous journeys
That is why they called me 'Moses'
Crossing rivers, sleeping in forests
Hiding by day, running by night
Charting our path to freedom by the sun and stars
Of course, the slave owners put a price on my head
It was a big price for someone so small
I was only five feet tall
Being small helped me to hide
It also helped me get through narrow openings
Soon, others who were helping slaves got to know
They provided me with food and shelter
We called it the 'Underground Railroad'
Once I had assembled a small group, we set out
Always under the cover of dark
Through the hills and valleys, living rough
Avoiding villages and towns by going the long way round
It was slow, but better than being caught
Along the way, good people gave us shelter
Thomas Garrett was one amongst many
In all, I made 13 expeditions
I helped over 300 slaves to reach freedom in the north
One of them was my sister
During one trip, I learned my husband had remarried
Should I visit and make a scene?
I decided against it
Best to focus on my new life and work
There was no point in risking arrest
In 1850, the risks became higher
The Fugitive Slave Law was passed
It meant that anyone aiding a slave's escape could be punished
Naturally, some people did not want to know us
A new escape route into Canada had to be arranged
It was also time to move on in other ways
Living in St Catherine's, Canada, was a safer spot for a while
It did not stop my activities to help slaves
The route was now well established, but dangerous

One special person who I rescued was my niece, Margaret
She was very close to me in all respects
In 1857, I made another special journey to Dorchester
It was to help my father escape
We celebrated with joy on crossing the border
John Brown, the abolitionist leader, called me 'General Tubman'
All around, people were talking about the slavery issue
Civil War was looming
The Southerners wanted to retain slavery
President Lincoln came to office to abolish it
It was not just a matter of slavery
It was about one country or two
To aid the cause, I volunteered for the Union Army
Initially, I worked as a cook
Then, when the battles were raging, I became a nurse
The injuries were horrific
Black soldiers or white, they still suffered the same
My reputation for helping slaves escape became known
Captain James Montgomery asked me to help in a different way
The Union Army wanted slaves to fight on their side
Therefore, I became a scout and a spy in enemy territory
Information on the location of Southern forces was gained
At the same time, I located slaves who wanted to escape
When I knew they would fight, I helped them
The Combahee River Expedition was an example
I was asked to find slaves who wanted to fight
By scouting ahead, I was in effect spying on the enemy
If caught, they would probably have killed me
However, my escape skills enabled me to report back
Three boats were sent to places that I indicated
With Union Army officials, we enabled 700 slaves to escape
More recruits for the battle
Once the war was over, I fought for equality
Not just for black people, but also for women's rights
That was my focus for the rest of my life
It was also a time that I found personal happiness
My first husband died in September 1867
I was now free in a different sense

Free to establish a new relationship
Nelson Davis was a soldier who I met in the Civil War
In his 30s, he was ten years younger than me
We got on well, as he understood and supported my work
On March 18th 1869, we married
Moving to Auburn, New York, we had 19 happy years
My work continued after his death
During that time, efforts were made to get me a pension
Mr Seward, a friend and politician, pressed the case
My claim was for three years as a cook and nurse
Also, my role as an army scout and spy
The time when I led a team of nine to gather information
Southern politicians voted against it for many years

HARRIET TUBMAN
1820-1913
THE "MOSES OF HER PEOPLE" HARRIET
TUBMAN OF THE BUCKTOWN DISTRICT
FOUND FREEDOM FOR HERSELF AND SOME
THREE HUNDRED OTHER SLAVES WHOM SHE
LED NORTH IN THE CIVIL WAR.

The war was won, but the battles continued
Eventually, in 1897, I was awarded 20 dollars a year
Recognition, after 32 years, for my work in the war
My other income was from a book written about my life
Reflecting on many amazing journeys
Remembering the different roles I had
Slave, wife, escapee, nurse, cook, scout, spy
Plus my work as a suffragette and author
Most of all, helping other slaves escape
In due course, I was able to set up a home for the elderly
One where I eventually resided
Reflecting on my life and the dreams I made come true.

Careers of Amazing Women

Today, many girls and women are pursuing careers in a way that would not have been possible in the past. Therefore, I thought it would be useful to review the achievements and recognition of the amazing women featured in this book in terms of what I regard as their main professional role. The women are icons of inspiration and show what can be achieved with determination and skill.

Each one of the women mentioned achieved important things in their lives. Some of them, like Marie Curie and Coco Chanel, have been commemorated and their names are relatively well-known. Others, like Susannah Holmes or Kato Shizue, are lesser-known and unsung heroines.

All of the women made a difference to the lives of others. Edith Piaf gave joy to many through her songs, albeit her own life was often one of sadness. Elizabeth Blackwell worked as a doctor, helping women and families in need. Maria Montessori devoted her life to help children develop their talents and abilities. Each one of these women showed what is possible through hard work in the pursuit of their ideas.

In the main, these women used their time well and their legacies are inspirational. We can all learn a great deal from the lives of these amazing women. This section of the book summarises the main areas of their contribution. It is complementary to the BioViews, which, by their nature, are an interpretation of what the women could have said if interviewed. These notes provide an indication of some of the facts and circumstances which led to the writing of the BioViews.

Areas of Contribution

Business Entrepreneur
Coco Chanel

Civil Rights Leader
Harriet Tubman

Colonial Mothers
Elizabeth Macarthur
Susannah Holmes

Chemist and Editor
Madame Lavoisier

Computer Specialist
Ada Lovelace

Doctor
Elizabeth Blackwell

Educator
Maria Montessori

Entertainer
Edith Piaf

Health Organisers
Kato Shizue
Mother Teresa

Mathematician and Editor
Emilie du Chatelet

Nurses
Edith Cavell
Florence Nightingale
Irene Sendler

Politicians
Nancy Astor
Golda Meir

Politician and Entertainer
Eva Peron

Scientist
Marie Curie

Secret Agent
Maria Poliakova

Slave
Sally Hemings

Slave and Civil Rights Leader
Sojourner Truth

Social Worker and Humanitarian
Caroline Chisholm

Women's Rights Activist
Emmeline Pankhurst

Business Entrepreneurs

Coco Chanel

Achievements

Born into a poor family, Coco was raised in a convent after her mother died and her father left. Her route from rags to riches was remarkable. She had the ability to identify and develop business opportunities. As a teenage girl she sang in nightclubs. Her other talent was making hats and she extended that to develop *haute couture*.

In 1913, she opened a shop in the centre of Paris, selling garments that had an appeal to those who wanted to stand out from the crowd. Film stars wore the hats she made and their pictures appeared in newspapers. It all helped raise the profile of Coco's work and the number of clients increased. With her business skills, she opened new shops in Deauville and Biarritz and eventually in other major cities across the world.

A major achievement was to commercialise her interest in garment design. She then extended her business into cosmetics and jewellery, which became an international business that brought her riches and fame. Coco had a long life and attracted considerable media attention, not just for her clothing designs but also her high profile social activities.

Recognition

Her name appears on shops in the main streets of the world's capital cities and in magazines advertising fashion. The Chanel organisation which she created lives on and maintains its position as one of the most prestigious fashion houses in the world.

Numerous books and films have been produced celebrating the life of Coco Chanel, particularly her social life, which was as scintillating as her business operations.

Civil Rights Leader

Harriet Tubman

Achievements

Harriet was named Araminta Ross, when born in 1822 into a Maryland family who were held in slavery. She was separated from her family and transferred on many occasions by the owners to work on various plantations before marrying John Tubman in 1844. After a hard life, she made a bid to escape in 1849. Her first attempt did not succeed. She made it on her second effort and eventually reached Philadelphia, where slavery had been abolished.

With bravery, she decided to return to help members of her family and others to escape. Through 13 dangerous rescue missions, she developed with others the so-called 'Underground Railroad' which was a series of 'safe houses' on the way to the northern States and Canada. She was given the nickname 'Moses', reflecting her efforts at leading her people from the wilderness.

She went on to campaign for women's rights, and became the first woman to lead an armed Union Army expedition. She is famed for the raid on the Combahee River, which resulted in the freeing of over 700 slaves. Harriet's concern for others led her into putting her own life at risk, when she could have enjoyed her freedom in safety.

When her first husband died, she found love with Nelson Davis, a Civil War veteran, and they enjoyed nearly 20 married years together. When she died, aged 91, Harriet was buried with military honours. Her life had reflected many roles from that of slave to Army scout and spy plus work as a nurse. Then she took on political roles as an orator and adviser to help abolish slavery.

Recognition

Harriet's gravestone is in Fort Hill Cemetery, Auburn, in Cayuga County (New York State). Erected in 1937 by the Empire State Federation of Women's Clubs, it is engraved with her married name of Harriet Tubman Davis. It is a tribute to her work both during the civil war and in freeing so many slaves. The granite structure is about three feet in height and is listed on the National Register of Historic Places.

The site of the raid on the Combahee River in South Carolina, which Harriet helped to orchestrate, is now marked by a bridge on US Highway 17.

Dorchester County, Maryland, where Harriet was born, is home to the 17 acre Harriet Tubman Underground Railroad State Park. The focus of the park is to commemorate Harriet and her life's achievements whilst preserving the environment and protecting wildlife. A National Park Service grant has been awarded to the park to improve outdoor recreational facilities. You may also wish to discover the routes she used to lead people away from slavery.

Colonial Mothers

Elizabeth Macarthur

Achievements

Sailing across the raging oceans of the world in 1790 was a frightening experience, particularly if you were pregnant. Elizabeth Macarthur was *en route* to the new British colony of New South Wales, Australia. She was accompanying her husband who was in the military corps. On arrival, Elizabeth set to work, amongst appalling poverty and disease, to help the new community. She not only contributed to that but also developed a farm to feed people and export sheep and wool back to Britain. In particular, she bred the world-renowned Merino sheep and was an entrepreneurial sheep industry founder.

Elizabeth was a founding mother of the new country. She had eight children, many of whom she did not see grow up, as they returned to England for their education. Her husband was also absent overseas for long periods. Elizabeth continued her farming work and developed the land, with the assistance of convicts and some free settlers. She was therefore a single mother for long periods and developed a career as a self-employed businesswoman.

Recognition

In 1937, the Macarthur Rose Garden was planted at Old Parliament House in Canberra to commemorate the contribution of Elizabeth and her husband to horticulture. Also of note is Elizabeth Macarthur High School situated at Narellan, a fast growing semi-rural area southwest of Sydney, Australia.

The building at 70 Alice Street, Rosehill, New South Wales is the site of the Macarthurs' original home. It is on the land called Elizabeth Farm. Construction started in 1793. It is the oldest European building that still exists in the region. Today, the building is a café that is open on weekends.

Susannah Holmes

Achievements

Susannah became a founding mother of Australia when she was sent to New South Wales as a convict for petty crime, in 1788. After marrying Henry Cable (Kable), they fought the first civil legal case in Australia and, against the odds, won. It was most unusual for a convict's word to be believed against a person of authority, such as the ship's captain whom she took to court.

It is thought likely that the expression to 'give someone a fair go', which is well known in Australia, arose from her action. Susannah Holmes won the case and was awarded 15 pounds in 1788. That was a huge sum at the time, albeit she could not spend it as she was a convict and there were no shops of note. Susannah gave birth to 11 children who became second-generation free native-born citizens of the Sydney colony which became in due course the new country of Australia.

Recognition

Apart from the legal records of 1788 in which her case is described in detail under her husband's name, Susannah Holmes, as far as we know, has not been publicly recognised by any memorial.

You can see reference to the July 1788 case at http://www.law.mq.edu.au.

The circumstances of her ordeal have been commemorated in a book called *The Transports: The Story of Australia's First Fleet* in the 25th Anniversary Edition of Peter Bellamy's Ballad Opera *The Transports* (Paperback) Publisher: Free Reed Music Ltd (1 Feb 2004) ISBN-10: 0954261046 / ISBN-13: 978-0954261047.

In addition, a book called *The Raking of the Embers* by June Whittaker, gives a fictional account of the times and circumstances of Susannah's life. ISBN 0207142068: 0207144435.

Many other books reflect the experiences of people like Susannah and two worthy of note are by Grace Karskens, entitled *The Colony*, ISBN / Catalogue Number: 9781742371023 and David Hill's book titled *1788*, ISBN / Catalogue Number: 9781741668001.

Susannah Holmes arrived at Botany Bay, south of Sydney, Australia. If you fly from overseas, this is close to the site of the Sydney International Airport, as well as many industrial organisations. However, Susannah did not step ashore at this point. Governor Philip felt the location would not support agricultural development and sent the convicts to Port Jackson instead, now known as Sydney.

Therefore, if you walk around The Rocks area of Sydney and out along Bennelong Point, towards the magnificent Opera House, you will be walking where Susannah Holmes once lived. It is also were she would have worked as a convict. Susannah raised her family of 11 children in the emerging Sydney Town. With the money awarded in the Court action, she and Henry became quite prosperous in the early days of the New South Wales colony, as it was known in those times.

Chemist and Editor

Madame Lavoisier

Achievements

Circumstances can change one's life and take it in a new direction. That happened twice to Marie-Anne Pierette Paulze, who became Madame Lavoisier. At the age of 13, she was living in a convent, as her mother had died. A rich man, who was about three times her age, made a proposal of marriage. To avoid this, her father approached a work colleague and asked him to marry his daughter. His name was Antoine Lavoisier and he agreed. In those days, arranged marriages were normal.

Marie-Anne and Antoine had little time to get to know each other before their marriage, but it proved a success. Antoine worked for the Government on tax issues, but spent as much time as possible on scientific experiments. Marie-Anne helped him by keeping notebooks and organizing the laboratory. Marie-Anne worked with Antoine on his 1789 publication of Lavoisier's Elementary Treatise on Chemistry, which presented a unified view of chemistry. As a gifted artist, she contributed thirteen sketch drawings.

It all seemed to be going well. However, 1789 was the year that the French Revolution turned life in Paris and France upside down. The aristocracy and previous Government officials were attacked and executed. Antoine Lavoisier was arrested and sent to the guillotine, along with many others, for no reason other than he had been part of the previous regime.

His wife pleaded for his release, but to no avail. However, she resolved to honour his memory by writing up his scientific works. Although the revolutionaries had taken his notebooks, she fought for their return. Then, she wrote one of the great works of science called *Mémoires de Chimie*. The first volume focused on issues of heat and the formation of liquids. The second volume dealt with the ideas of combustion, air, effects of air and liquids on metals, plus the action of acids, and the composition of water.

Recognition

The work of Antoine Lavoisier is now known around the world. However, it is only because of his wife, Marie-Anne, that we have the records. Most of these are housed in the Cornell University Library in the USA.

During her life, Marie-Anne received little or no recognition. It was the Time of Terror, when people were killed if the revolutionaries thought they were a danger. After the revolutionaries Napoleon's armies came marching across Europe.

It was difficult for women to be recognized for any professional work. They were expected to stay at home and have a family. It is only in recent times that the work of Madame Lavoisier has been given more prominence. She has been called the Mother of Modern Chemistry.

Computer Specialist

Ada Lovelace

Achievements

Ada was the daughter of Lord Byron, who left his family when Ada was very young. Her mother imposed strong discipline upon Ada and she became a gifted mathematician. On meeting Charles Babbage, she realised that her skills could assist him in his computer development work. As a result, during a nine month period in 1842-43, Lovelace translated Italian mathematician Luigi Menabrea's memoir on Babbage's proposed machine, the Analytical Engine. She then added her own views on computer applications and is thought to have been the first computer programmer. It was groundbreaking work and set the scene for those who were to follow by leaving a record of what had been done.

Recognition

There was little or no recognition of Ada in her own lifetime. She regarded it as unfeminine to sign her name to the papers that she wrote, as women were expected to concentrate on domestic matters. Therefore, she only put her initials on the papers that were published.

In 1953, over 100 years after her death, Lovelace's notes on Babbage's Analytical Engine were re-published. That engine is now recognised as an early model for a computer.

The USA Defence Department named the computer language *Ada* after Ada Lovelace. The reference manual for the language was approved on 10th December 1980, and the number associated with it was the year of her birth.

In addition, Lovelace's image can be seen on the Microsoft product authenticity hologram stickers. Since 1998, the British Computer Society has awarded a medal in Ada's name and in 2008 initiated an annual competition for female students of Computer Science.

In the popular media, Lovelace has been portrayed in the novel *The Difference Engine*, by William Gibson and Bruce Sterling.

Doctor

Elizabeth Blackwell

Achievements

Elizabeth was the first female doctor to qualify at an American medical school, even though her applications were rejected 17 times before she gained entry. She then travelled to England and became the first female doctor accepted on the British Medical Register. With Elizabeth Garret and others, she pioneered the development of health care for women and trained many female doctors.

Recognition

Elizabeth did not seek public recognition, however the Hobart and William Smith Colleges (previously Geneva Medical College) where she studied, founded an Elizabeth Blackwell Award during the 1950s. The award is given annually to women who are considered to have made outstanding contributions to humanity. There is a monument with a sculpture of Elizabeth at this institution.

In New York, Elizabeth founded a hospital and trained women doctors. Although it closed in 1899, the hospital she founded, now vastly enlarged and renamed New York Infirmary-Strang Clinic, still operates on East 15th Street.

An original monument to her memory has been erected at Asheville, North Carolina in the United States. It is on the side of the Wachovia Bank Building on Patton Avenue, just across the street from the Drhumor Building.

In London, the Wellcome Historical Medical Museum in Wigmore Street provides the context within which Elizabeth Blackwell contributed to the development of medical practice in Britain.

High on the wall of Rock House, Exmouth Place in Hastings, England, is a white memorial tablet to Elizabeth who lived in the house for 30 years, from 1879 until her death in 1910.

Educator

Maria Montessori

Achievements

Born in Italy, Maria's initial ambition was to be an engineer. However, that was difficult in a society ruled by men and the Catholic Church, both of whom tended to expect women to focus on family duties. She changed her field of study and qualified as the first female doctor in her country. Specialising in psychiatry, she recognised that many children had learning difficulties. She developed her own approach, known worldwide as the Montessori Method. Her philosophy was to 'Educate for Peace' and the first Montessori school opened in 1907.

She wrote a number of books on her approach including the following:

- Montessori, Maria: The Discovery of the Child ISBN 0-345-33656-9
- Montessori, Maria: The Montessori Method ISBN 0-8052-0922-0

- Montessori, Maria: The Secret of Childhood ISBN 0-345-30583-3

Recognition

The Opera Nazionale Montessori (ONM) was set up as a moral organisation and legal entity by Royal Decree no. 1534, on 8 August 1924. Based in Rome, it is the heir and repository of a specific scientific educational and pedagogic tradition and also a national organisation for research, experimentation, training, assistance, consultancy, promotion and dissemination for Montessorian scientific and methodological principles and ideals.

The Association Montessori Internationale (see http://www.montessori-ami. org) was founded in 1929 by Maria to maintain the integrity of her life's work, and to ensure that it would be perpetuated after her death.

Entertainer

Edith Piaf

Achievements

The distinctive singing voice of Edith Piaf has become known throughout the world. She had the ability to touch people's emotions through her singing, particularly in her signature song *Non, Je Ne Regrette Rien*. Indeed, the song reflected her philosophy of experience, as she rose from being a street urchin to a superstar of theatre and radio. Along the way, there were many dramatic difficulties, but Edith continued to triumph over the despair and tragic circumstances of her life.

It was on the stage that Edith shone, whether it was an improvised street pavement, at the Olympia in Paris, or at the concert halls of New York, London, and Rome. Her vibrant voice sold millions of records. It should have made her very rich, but her lifestyle was one of 'spend and enjoy the moment'. In due course, she became dependent on drugs and the money disappeared into the pockets of those who supplied her.

Recognition

Edith's many hit songs brought her acclaim and recognition in many countries. Within her own country, France, she became an icon for many young people who identified with her music and perhaps her lifestyle.

In 1947, Edith decided to sail to New York. The 31year old had cultivated a unique onstage presence, and became a huge star there, regularly appearing on *The Ed Sullivan Show* and at Carnegie Hall. The people of the United States recognised Edith as a star.

According to legend, Piaf was born as Edith Giovanna Gassion on the pavement outside 72 rue de Belleville, Paris in the depth of winter - attested to by a plaque outside the door. Nearby, a statue depicts Edith Piaf's early years as a street singer in Belleville. However, Piaf's birth certificate states that she was born at the Hospital Tenon, perhaps where her mother, Annette Maillard, a café singer, was taken when found giving birth to Edith in the street. The certificate is on display at the Edith Piaf Museum, two rooms of memorabilia in a Belleville apartment belonging to Bernard Marchois, the author of several Piaf biographies.

Edith worked with a writer to produce her autobiography *Au Bal de la Chance* (*Wheel of Fortune*) in 1958. Her childhood home, on rue Crespin Gu Gast in Paris, is now a private museum dedicated to the life and music of the star. On display are the singer's photographs, jewellery, furniture, and other memorabilia. Her place of burial, located at Cimetière du Père Lachaise, Paris, France, Plot: Division 97, is regarded by some as a shrine.

Health Organisers

Kato Shizue

Achievements

Respect for tradition in Japan has always been strong and, until recently, women were not supposed to 'interfere' in business or politics. Indeed, married women were expected to focus on their roles as wives and mothers. That is what Kato Shizue did in her early years.

However, she observed the problems of other women who had little information and advice on health issues and decided to assist. While visiting the USA she met Margaret Sange, who campaigned for birth control and women's health issues. On returning to Japan, Kato Shizue established clinics for women, but hostility from many politicians and many men hindered her. For example, in 1927, the Government imprisoned her for opposing its plan to expand the population.

It was after the Second World War that she was able to make progress. Japan had been badly defeated and food was scarce. Politicians realised the need for birth control for economic, rather than health, reasons. Also, Kato Shizue took the opportunity provided by the new democratic processes and was elected to the Japanese Diet (Parliament). She served for 28 years from 1946 to 1974, which is an amazing achievement in itself.

Her work focused particularly on women's issues. In 1948, she co-founded the Japan Family Planning Association. Despite the difficulties, it survived and now planned parenthood is an accepted part of education for women.

Recognition

In 1984, she received the United Nation's Population Award, which was an acknowledgement amongst world leaders of her contribution to education for women on those issues.

The Kato Shizue Award, founded in 1996, "targets women's groups, women's organisations and/or individual women who are active in the movement toward improvement of sexual and reproductive health/rights of women. It also encourages the empowerment of women in social, economic, political and legal issues in developing countries and/or in Japan."

In 1997, Kato Shizue celebrated her 100th birthday. A programme on Japanese television told the remarkable story of her life and reflected the ways in which people had recognised her contribution to women's health.

Mother Teresa

Achievements

Deciding to leave home in Skopje, Macedonia, and go to Ireland to train as a nun, was an enormous step for a young girl who did not speak English and who had never travelled abroad before. They were the first steps that Agnesë Gonxhe Bojaxhiu made in her quest to help people in need. That was the family name of Mother Teresa.

After training in Ireland, she went to India. For over 45 years, she tended the sick and destitute. To do this, she left the confines of the convent and her teaching job to work in the streets and camps where the poor lived. Missionaries of Charity, the organisation she established, grew in size and eventually became an international organisation to help those in need.

She gained world recognition for her charity work and in 1982 went to Beirut to help rescue 37 children caught in a war battleground. Visits to Ethiopia, the Chernobyl nuclear disaster site and to earthquake victims in Armenia followed. Hers was a life given to helping others survive and improving their living conditions.

Recognition

Mother Teresa's life is, and has been, celebrated in many countries including the Philippines, Italy, India, Australia, the United Kingdom and the United States.

Pope John XXIII awarded her a Peace Prize and she later received the Pacem in Terris Award.

Many universities raced to award her honorary degrees. She also gained the United States Presidential Medal of Freedom (1985) and the Congressional Gold Medal (1994).

Mother Teresa was awarded the Templeton Prize in 1973, and India's highest civilian award, the Bharat Ratna in 1980. In 1996, The United States made her an Honorary Citizen (one of only six).

In 1979, she was awarded the Nobel Peace Prize. Pope John Paul II beatified her in October 2003 so Catholics may properly call her Blessed Teresa.

She was the first and only person featured on an Indian postage stamp while still alive. In 1972, Mother Teresa received the Nehru Prize for her promotion of international peace and understanding.

Mother Teresa is recognised for her books about Christian spirituality and prayer, some of which were written with her close friend Frère Roger.

Other awards included the Balzan prize in 1978 for humanity, peace and goodwill among peoples and the Albert Schweitzer International Prize (1975).

There was no shortage of recognition for her work, although some criticism was made of her methods and processes.

Mathematician and Editor

Emilie du Chatelet

Achievements

Being born into a French aristocratic family enabled Emilie to gain a solid education. By the age of 12, she spoke Latin, German, Italian and Greek and had started to study English. However, at the time, it was not expected that females needed, or would use, the knowledge and skills gained. So it appeared to be in the case of Emilie. She entered an arranged marriage in June 1725 and became the Marquise du Chastellet. With her husband, a military man, she had three children. It looked and seemed a conventional kind of life.

However, Emilie wanted more excitement than just being a wife and mother. No doubt an attractive woman, she had affairs while her husband was away on military duty. The fourth was with Voltaire, the celebrated French writer. He called her Madame du Châtelet in public and that name has become recognised as her professional *nom de plume*. Voltaire encouraged her to develop talents and explore physics and mathematics. She did so and published scientific articles and translations.

In 1737, Emilie published a paper entitled *Dissertation sur la nature et la propagation du feu*, a scientific study of fire, predicting what we know as infrared radiation. Her book *Institutions de Physique* (*Lessons in Physics*) was published in 1740, giving an overview of new ideas in science and philosophy to be studied by her 13 year-old son.

Emilie du Châtelet was an original thinker and supported her ideas with experiments. Her most original contribution was to identify energy with $mv2$. She proposed that energy was conserved, and that one form of energy might be converted to another, but that the total energy was constant. This challenged Newton's ideas as he argued that mv, a scalar quantity that he observed, could disappear in a collision.

Emilie had exceptional abilities. One of them was interpreting the works of others. Her lasting fame came from a translation of Isaac Newton's great book on mathematics. Emilie made the full text available to French scholars in their own language. Over 250 years later, Emilie du Châtelet's translation of *Principia Mathematica* is still the standard translation of the work in French.

Recognition

Because of her well-known affairs in French high society Emilie had a reputation. Perhaps it distracted from her being taken seriously as a scholar. Indeed, few if any women were considered to be scholars. Therefore, she was not accepted into the great academies or given any honours.

It was only after her early death, during her 40s, that people began to consider the legacy she had left. Voltaire, her lover, sang her praises but once again there was little recognition. However, the written work began to speak for itself, as scholars realised the value of her insights and contributions.

The fact that her interpretation of Newton's work is still in print and re-published from generation to generation keeps her name alive. Today, Emilie is regarded as one of France's most original thinkers and contributors to academic development.

A crater on Venus has been named in her honour.

Nurses

Edith Cavell

Achievements

In 1914, the Germans invaded Belgium as well as other countries as they raced westwards to the English Channel. Britain sent troops to defend the people of the invaded countries. The battles were brutal and the war took the lives of millions of people. One of them was Edith Cavell, assassinated by the Germans in cold blood.

Born in England in 1865, she was an accomplished linguist, musician and artist. Having trained as a nurse in London, she went to work in Belgium before the war. When the war began, she was in England caring for her family. She could have avoided the direct conflict of the war but instead she bravely volunteered to return to Belgium and the front line of the battle.

The Germans took over the hospital where she was in a senior role caring for the wounded of both sides. They alleged that she was helping allied soldiers escape, put her on trial, convicted and executed her. Her achievements in helping the wounded of both sides did not stop them murdering Edith, whose mission in life was to help heal those who were sick and injured.

Recognition

Many memorials have been built to commemorate Edith's life and work. One was unveiled in October 1918 in the grounds of Norwich Cathedral, near a home for nurses which also bore her name.

Other memorials include:

•   a stone memorial, including a statue of Cavell, adjacent to Trafalgar Square in London

•   a memorial in Peterborough Cathedral, England

•   an inscription on a war memorial, naming the 35 people executed by the German army outside the jail in which they were killed

•   a dedication on the war memorial on the grounds of Sacred Trinity

Church, Salford, England

A number of medical facilities commemorate her name and include:

- Edith Cavell Hospital in Peterborough, where she received part of her education
- Edith Cavell Clinic, Brussels, Belgium
- Cavell Building, Quinte Children's Treatment Centre, Belleville, Ontario, Canada, as well as wings of other hospitals
- University of East Anglia, Norwich, England, named its School of Nursing and Midwifery centre the Edith Cavell Building, when it opened in 2006

Many schools have commemorated her memory and there are other mentions of her name including:

- Cavell Gardens, Inverness, Scotland
- Mount Edith Cavell, a peak in the Canadian Rockies, named in 1916
- Cavell Corona, a geological feature on Venus
- The Edith Cavell Nursing Scholarship Fund, a philanthropy of the Dallas County Medical Society Alliance Foundation, provides scholarships to exceptional nursing students in Dallas, Texas, USA
- There is a hospital in the Brussels borough of Uccle named after her
- A bridge in Queenstown, New Zealand, and a guest house in Clevedon, Somerset (Cavell House), where she spent some of her childhood
- Radio Cavell 1350 am, broadcasting to the staff and patients on The Royal Oldham Hospital Charity Radio

Australians raised considerable money to perpetuate Edith's memory. In 1916, the Edith Cavell Trust Fund, officially inaugurated in Victoria, lasted nearly 60 years, until 1974. Her memorial still stands at the Melbourne, Victoria, Shrine of Remembrance. In New South Wales, a 'rest home' for nurses returning from both World Wars was established. The NSW Nurses' Association, found another significant and enduring way to commemorate Edith Cavell through The Edith Cavell Trust, established in 1992 to support nursing research and nurse education.

Florence Nightingale

Achievements

Early in her life, Florence made a decision to dedicate her life to try and save the lives of others. She wrote that her God had spoken to her and made it clear what was required. From that day on, she focused on helping those in need. Despite opposition from her wealthy parents, Florence set forth to work with the poor and needy. She left her substantial home at Embley Park, Romsey, Hampshire (now a school) and started to train as a nurse, both in England and Germany.

The Crimean War brought her to prominence. She arranged for 38 women to travel to the battlefront, at Scutari, to nurse and assist the wounded. Despite opposition from both the military and medical sector, she persevered and became known as the 'Lady of the Lamp' as she toured the makeshift hospital facilities at night.

On her return, she set to work advising the British Government. She had a number of influential friends and apart from meeting senior politicians to influence Parliament, she was invited to conduct research on the requirements to improve health in the country.

In response to an invitation from Queen Victoria's Government, Florence was a major player on the Health of the Army Royal Commission, with Sidney Herbert as the Chairman. As a woman, Nightingale could not be appointed to the Commission, but she wrote the 1000-plus page report and *Notes on Matters Affecting the Health, Efficiency and Hospital Administration of the British Army*. The report and notes led to a major overhaul of army military care, to the establishment of an Army Medical School and of a comprehensive system of army medical records.

In 1859, 45,000 pounds received from the Nightingale Fund was used to set up the Nightingale Training School at St Thomas' Hospital on 9 July 1860. It is now called the Florence Nightingale School of Nursing and Midwifery and is part of the University of London King's College. The first trained Nightingale nurses began work on 16 May 1865 at the Liverpool Workhouse Infirmary.

Florence wrote many documents including *Notes on Nursing*, published in 1860. She spent the rest of her life promoting the establishment and development of the nursing profession and organising it into its modern form.

In 1869, Nightingale and Dr Elizabeth Blackwell opened the Women's Medical College in London. In addition, in the 1870s, Nightingale mentored Linda Richards, America's first trained nurse, who established high-quality nursing schools.

In her later life, Nightingale made a comprehensive statistical study of sanitation in Indian rural life and was the leading figure in the introduction of improved medical care and public health service in India.

She also found time to write various works including *Cassandra* in 1851, and *Suggestions for Thought (to Searchers after Religious Truth)*, *Mysticism and Eastern Religions*, *Florence Nightingale's Theology* and *Florence Nightingale's Spiritual Journey*.

Recognition

On 29 November 1855, a public meeting voted to give recognition to Florence Nightingale for her work in the war and led to the establishment of the Nightingale Fund for the training of nurses.

In 1859, Nightingale was elected the first female member of the Royal Statistical Society and she later became an honorary member of the American Statistical Association.

In 1883, Nightingale was awarded the Royal Red Cross by Queen Victoria. In 1907, she became the first woman to receive the Order of Merit and she was given the Honorary Freedom of the City of London in 1908,

Four hospitals in Istanbul, Turkey are named after Florence Nightingale.

A statue of Florence Nightingale stands in Waterloo Place, Westminster, London, near the Mall. Also in London, there is the Florence Nightingale Museum and another one devoted to her at Claydon House, her sister's family home.

There are three statues of Florence Nightingale in Derby: one outside the Derby Royal Infirmary, one in St. Peter's Street, and one above the Nightingale-Macmillan Continuing Care Unit opposite the Derby Royal Infirmary. A public house named after her stands close to the Derby Royal Infirmary. In addition, there are many roads and schools named in her honour.

Irena Sendler

Achievements

We can all wonder what we would do if confronted with dilemma of helping other people when doing so would jeopardise your own life. That is what happened to Irena Sendler or, as she was known in her native Poland, Irena Sendlerowa. Born in 1910, she lived through difficult times leading up to and including the German invasion of Poland in 1939 and the Nazi determination to kill the Jews.

Living in Warsaw, Irena, who was a nurse and social worker, witnessed what was happening in the ghetto. She had special access as a health worker and decided to risk her own life time after time in order to rescue Jewish children. 'Zegota' was the name given to an underground organisation assisting Jewish people. Irena joined it and was given the codename 'Jolanta'.

Over months, she constructed a trusted network of people who were willing to help her. After smuggling children from the ghetto, she placed them with priests, nuns and local families who offered to help. The names of the children were kept in a jar under the soil in her garden. In 1943, Irena was arrested and tortured by the Nazis, who then condemned her to death. The Zegota organisation members had bribed a German officer to spare her life by leaving her unconscious in a field where her friends found her. They took her to a safe place where she recovered from her injuries. It is estimated that about 2500 children were saved through her efforts.

Recognition

The Yad Vashem Holocaust Memorial Centre in Jerusalem is a huge site containing the Holocaust History Museum and memorial sites such as the Children's Memorial. The centre is dedicated to research, education, commemoration and documentation of the Holocaust, and hosts many events and exhibitions. In 1965, Irena was recognised by Yad Vashem as one of the 'Righteous Among the Nations'. It is an honour awarded to non-Jewish people who saved the lives of Jewish people during the Holocaust. A tree has been planted in her honour and stands at the entrance to the Avenue of the Righteous Among the Nations.

In 2003, Irena received Poland's highest civil decoration, which is called the 'Order of the White Eagle'. In Washington, she was given the Jan Karski Award 'For Courage and Heart' by the American Center of Polish Culture.

Poland's Senate honoured Irena in 2007. By that time, she was 97 years of age and too frail in health to go to the ceremony. In the same year, she was given the 'Order of the Smile Award' for contributions to the love and care of children. However, Irena's amazing contributions were little known outside of Poland until 2006 when Anna Mieszkowska published a book , *The Mother of the Holocaust Children*. The next year, four students at Uniontown, Kansas, heard of Irena and researched her work. They wrote a play called *Life in a Jar*. Initially, it was performed locally at a number of schools, but became known and led to recognition across the USA. They visited Poland to meet Irena before she died in 2008 at the age of 98.

Politicians

Nancy Astor

Achievements

Born in the USA, Nancy Astor became the first woman to take a seat in the British Parliament and she was a member for over 25 years.

Both her parents and her husband were extremely rich, but Nancy had more than that – she had the ability to influence and persuade people through her powerful speeches. Behind closed doors, she wielded considerable influence on politicians and business people by hosting grand dinners and society gatherings at her Cliveden Estate.

During wartime, Nancy converted her large home into a hospital for wounded soldiers and helped them recover.

Recognition

The Cliveden Estate was the family home of Waldorf and Nancy Astor. They lived in the magnificent house for many years and it was later given to the National Trust. It can be visited at Taplow, Maidenhead, Buckinghamshire.

Nancy's contribution to British politics is recognised in various education courses on politics and, increasingly, in courses related to women's studies.

Golda Meir

Achievements

For someone born into poverty, amongst the persecuted Jews of the Ukraine, Golda Meir had a remarkable life. Her family immigrated to the USA, where she was educated. With a burning passion to represent Jewish people, she went to Israel and became the first female Prime Minister of the country. She was the third woman to hold such an office from all countries. *En route*, she had many high level jobs, including that of Israeli ambassador to Russia.

Golda Meir married and had a family, but her wider family was the political group that sought to establish the nation state of Israel. She became a member of the Histadrut, the powerful leadership organisation. The Government of Israel appointed Golda as both Minister of Labour and Foreign Minister. In 1948, she went to the United States and managed to raise 50,000,000 dollars, which was used to purchase arms in Europe for the nascent state. On another occasion, she dressed in the garb of an Arab woman to travel in secret across Jordan, where she negotiated with the King on the future of Israel.

During her time as Prime Minister of Israel, she was known as the Iron Lady. That quality was displayed in her contributions during the Six Day War with Arab countries. However, she also fought for peace. In 1969, she met with world leaders to try to establish peace in the Middle East region.

Recognition

In 1975, Golda Meir was awarded the Israeli Prize for her special contribution to the State of Israel. In the same year she also published her autobiography *My Life*.

The memory and contribution of Golda Meir is commemorated in many ways and the following only represent a few of the places which people can visit:

- Golda Meir School, Milwaukee, Wisconsin.
- Golda Meir Library, University of Wisconsin-Milwaukee, Wisconsin
- Golda Meir Boulevard, Jerusalem, Israel
- Golda Meir Center for the Performing Arts, Tel Aviv
- Golda Meir Square, New York City
- Golda Meir Center for Political Leadership at Metropolitan State College Of Denver
- Golda Meir House, Denver, Colorado

Politician and Entertainer

Eva Peron

Achievements

Eva was born Eva Duarte, the last of five children, as a result of an affair between her mother and a wealthy rancher, Juan Darte. He deserted Eva and her mother to return to his wife in a nearby city. Eva's mother was left with no support, and so sewed clothes for villagers, as well as taking in boarders to pay the bills. Eva learned a lot by meeting the different people who stayed at her home. She was also sent to school, where she realised her interests lay with the arts, and becoming an actress.

At the young age of 15, Eva travelled to Buenos Aires. Staying with friends of her father, she worked where she could during the day and joined theatrical groups at night. In 1935, Eva began her acting career at the Comedias Theatre in a piece called *The Perezes Misses*. At 17, Eva appeared in a B-grade film and travelled Argentina with a theatre group.

After acting in a daily drama series on Radio El Mundo, Eva was offered a five year contract with Radio Belgrano. As a part of the Great Women of History series, Eva played the roles of Elizabeth I of England and the last

Tsarina of Russia, amongst others. Soon she was able to buy shares in the company and pay for an apartment of her own in one of the better areas of Buenos Aires.

National politics began to interest Eva, and the Argentine Radio Syndicate (ARA) was formed. In 1944, an earthquake tragedy struck San Juan, Argentina. Thousands were killed and injured. An artistic festival was organised by the Secretary of Labour, Juan Peron. Eva met Peron at party gala. It was the start of a powerful relationship. With 25 years separating their ages, and living together unmarried, many disapproved. But they had similar interests and supported each other. Eva helped Peron to become President of Argentina, and he in turn helped Eva to become President of the Actor's Union.

Eva supported Peron and his campaign through her radio broadcasts. However, Peron's opponents arrested him and placed him in jail. Eva organised a peaceful protest march against his imprisonment. Over 30,000 people marched, demanding the release of Peron. Within two days, Peron was pardoned. A day later, Eva and Peron married in celebration of his release.

Eva began speaking on the campaign trail, raising awareness of women in politics along the way. Juan Peron was elected President of Argentina in 1946. Eva took a tour of Europe, where there was much poverty and devastation as a result of World War II. She met many influential people, including the Pope and the President of France, but was not asked to meet senior people in Britain. 'The Rainbow Tour' ended and Eva returned to Argentina.

There, she founded the Eva Peron Foundation. Horse racing, casinos and lotteries all helped to raise funds. Soon the Foundation had over 200 million dollars and employed over 14,000 people. Hospitals and schools were built, shoes and cooking utensils were supplied, and Evita City was built to help with the housing crisis. Eva met with many sick and needy people, including those whom society shunned. Her days were busy and Eva was soon working 20 hours a day, trying to fit everything in.

With the help of Peron, women were given the right to vote. Eva formed the Female Peronist Party and by 1951 there were 500,000 members. Peron was elected into office again, and Eva was offered the role of Vice President, which she declined. Soon after, Eva began losing energy and, after fainting during a meeting, was told she had cervical cancer. Eva underwent a radical hysterectomy, but it was to no avail. At the age of 33, after an amazing life as an entertainer and politician, Eva passed away. She is remembered as one of the most influential politicians in Argentina. Her tireless work encouraged women to be treated as equals and raised awareness of the poverty problem in her own country and throughout the world.

Recognition

During her tour of Europe, Eva was awarded the Cross of Isabel the Catholic, by the Spanish Government. In 1952, Eva was named Spiritual Leader of the Nation by the Argentine Congress.

On the day of Eva's death, Argentina went into mourning. All activity in the country was suspended for two days and the national flag was flown at half mast for ten days. Eva was honoured with a State funeral, despite never taking office as a head of state. Eva's coffin was laid to rest in the Duarte family mausoleum in La Recoleta Cemetery in Buenos Aires.

Her husband commissioned a monument to be built in her honour after her death. Work commenced on the monument, but after Peron was forced into exile, the monument was destroyed, along with all other buildings and organisations associated with Eva and the Perons.

The date of Eva's death is marked annually by Argentineans, despite not being designated as an official holiday. Eva's face has been featured on a number of Argentinean coins. Evitas were named in honour of Eva. Evita City is located just outside of Buenos Aires.

In 2002, Museo Evita was opened in Buenos Aires in honour of the 50th anniversary of Eva's passing. The Evita Peron Historical Research Foundation (www.evaperon.org) was established in 1998 by her family, with the aim of providing information about Eva and her life.

Many books, doctorates and plays have been written about Eva's life, including investigative reports into her political dealings, and those of her husband. Perhaps the most well-known representation of Eva's life is the musical *Evita*. This was eventually remade as a movie, starring pop singer Madonna. The Argentine government later released *Eva Peron: The True Story* in response to *Evita*.

Scientist

Marie Curie

Achievements

Marie Curie was born during 1859 in Vistula Country, which was part of the then Russian Empire. Her given name was Maria Sklodowska. She was the fifth and youngest child of a proud Polish family. Their country had been invaded, not for the first or indeed the last time. Therefore, her early life was difficult in more senses than one.

After leaving school, she took various jobs to help pay for her sister to go to France to gain a university education. Entry for women into Polish universities was barred. Higher education was reserved for men only. Maria therefore joined the so-called 'Floating University' in Warsaw. This was like a secret underground group of young people and more experienced Polish people who shared knowledge and ideas.

In 1891, after great efforts, she joined her sister in Paris and went to Sorbonne University. It was the start of a new life, speaking and learning a new language, and the beginning of a remarkable career that led her to win two Nobel Prizes. She is the only woman to have done so.

During her research, she met Pierre Curie, another scientist. In 1895, they married. That is how Maria became known as Marie Curie, a French citizen from Poland. Their joint work led to the discovery of polonium, which Marie named after Poland and radium, as a result of the radioactivity it generated.

During the First World War, Marie Curie established mobile radiography units to gain X-rays of injuries to help the treatment of injured soldiers. The gold that she gained from the Nobel Prize was given to the French war effort in their fight against the Germans.

The Curie name was also used in a process to treat some cancers, and became known as 'Curie Therapy'. Marie had two daughters, one of whom was also awarded a Nobel Prize for physics and the other wrote her biography.

Recognition

Firstly, Marie was not recognised by the Académie Française. They did not elect her into membership, maybe because she was not a native-born French person or maybe because she was a woman.

Marie however gained many other honours and worldwide recognition. In Paris, she became the leader of the prestigious Pasteur Institute and a radioactivity laboratory at the University of Paris.

Her two Nobel Prizes, gained in 1903 and 1911, were in different fields. The publicity brought her to the attention of politicians and academics around the world. In addition, she was awarded the Davy Medal in the UK during 1903 and the Matteucci Medal, in Italy in 1904.

Madame Curie was decorated with the French Legion D'Honneur. In Poland, she established the Curie Institute for research and a monument to her memory stands in front of the building. In 1967, a museum devoted to the work of Maria Sklodowska, as she is known in Poland, was established in Warsaw's New Town at her birthplace on Freta Street.

Secret Agent

Maria Poliakova

Achievements

Maria Poliakova was a member of the Russian intelligence. During the Second World War, she orchestrated 'Gisela's Family' – a ring of spies containing influential figures from the German Army and Foreign Office. The key to the success of this spy ring was the mysterious 'Werther' (now widely believed to have been Martin Bormann). Werther's position close to Hitler ensured accurate information was procured and directly helped the Soviet fight against Hitler's forces. Maria's love for her people inspired her great courage, which contributed to the defeat of the Nazis.

Recognition

As Maria's work was 'below the radar' it is difficult to find places to which she is linked. However she did spend time working at the Kremlin, and this is where the intelligence she gathered would have been directed.

Standing on the banks of the Moskva River, the Kremlin is a UNESCO World Heritage Site. It is a fortified complex containing four palaces and four cathedrals, and is the official residence of the Russian President. The Moscow State Historical and Cultural Museum is contained within the Ivan the Great Bell Tower, and tells the story of the Kremlin from its earliest developments and offers a bird's eye view of the Kremlin site from the upper gallery of the tower.

Slave

Sally Hemings

Achievements

In colonial times, there were few opportunities for women to gain an education, to travel or to work in a career outside the home. For a slave girl it was even worse, as they were tied to the plantation of their owner.

Sally Hemings was a slave, but she did travel to France and lived in a grand house there. While in France, she was taught various domestic skills, but no doubt acquired a working knowledge of the French language. In addition, she learnt a lot about French life and what it was like to live under a system where she was not a slave. In her role as a maid and companion to Mary, the daughter of Thomas Jefferson, she would have discussed with her what she was learning and probably learnt to read and write at a basic level.

The story of Sally Hemings is based partly on the facts and partly on assumptions. It is known that she went to England and then to France. She was accompanying Mary, Jefferson's daughter, who was eight years old. It is known that she lived at the Hotel de Langeac, a substantial home (not actually a hotel) on the Champs Elysees. This was the residence of Jefferson, who was the American ambassador to France.

The evidence indicates that Sally was paid a wage while in France. She was probably paid by Jefferson himself, or was an employee of the US Government. It also indicates that she was not regarded as a slave during this time. The fact that she was paid a wage gave her some independence not afforded to slaves in Virginia.

It is also known that Jefferson paid to buy her new dresses. Based on this fact, certain assumptions can be made. Jefferson was invited to many social functions and would have been expected to be accompanied on some, if not all, of them. Would he have chosen someone from outside his own group or invited someone whom he knew?

What sort of a life did Sally Hemings have in France? That is not recorded in detail, but there is some evidence that while there she had a relationship and conceived. On her return to America, the baby died. It has been suggested that Thomas Jefferson was the father. Indeed, Sally Hemings had five other children and the evidence suggests that Jefferson was the father of those children also. Therefore, it is possible that he and Sally Hemings began a relationship in Paris which continued when they returned to Monticello, his mansion in Virginia.

Sally is reported to have had a room of her own in Jefferson's house and to have been engaged as a house servant. Of course, on her return to Virginia, Sally Hemings was once again a slave under the law.

Jefferson went on to become the President of the United States of America and could have put forward a law to abolish slavery. He did not do so. Abraham Lincoln did that and slavery was officially abolished in 1865. Therefore, when Sally Hemings died in 1835, she was still officially labelled a slave under the law of the time. Also, although she had six children there is no record to indicate that she married.

Recognition

For many years, the facts of the case were ignored or covered up. That is interesting as James T. Callender, a journalist, made allegations at the time about the relationship between Jefferson and Hemings. The allegations were fuelled by the fact that Jefferson had not appointed him to be the Postmaster of Richmond, Virginia. This may seem to be just small town politics, but the allegations were very dangerous for Jefferson, who was seeking election as President of the USA.

Therefore, the first recognition of Sally Hemings emerged as a result of ill feelings by James Callender. The innuendo and embarrassing allegations faded away when Callender was found dead in 1803. He had drowned in about two feet of water. It was said that he was drunk at the time and no allegations of foul play were made.

In due course, the children of Sally Hemings grew up. Interestingly, Jefferson arranged for them to gain their freedom. Harriet was allowed to leave Monticello in 1822. Sally's sons, Madison and Eston, were freed in the Will of Jefferson. The other children died when young. In contrast, he did not free any other slaves.

Eston changed his name to Eston Hemings Jefferson in 1852. Madison declared in 1873 that Thomas Jefferson was his father and also of his brothers and sisters. All of these statements gave more credence to the story first published by James T. Callender.

Within the last decade, there has been more recognition of the issues. Following substantial scientific research involving DNA testing, a report was written by the Research Committee on Thomas Jefferson and Sally Hemings. In January 2000, it concluded that there was a high level of probability that Thomas Jefferson was indeed the father of Sally Hemings' children.

Subsequently, there have been a number of books and documentaries made about the life of Sally Hemings giving further recognition to this assumption. However, as far as is known, there are no monuments or other public recognitions of her life and contribution. Perhaps there should be, as she was the first African American mother who lived with, and gave birth to the sons and daughters of, an American President.

Slave and Civil Rights Leader

Sojourner Truth

Achievements

Sojourner Truth was one of 13 children in her family who were enslaved in Ulster County, New York, where Dutch was the common language. Therefore, she grew up speaking that language until she was sold at an auction when nine years old, to John Neely. It must have been a traumatic experience. She was sold again in 1808 when she was 11 years old and again in 1810. In about the year 1815, whilst still enslaved, Sojourner wanted to marry a slave from a different plantation. However, the owners forbade it and she was forced into an arranged marriage instead which resulted in her having six children, one of whom died shortly after the birth. In 1826, as a mark of her independence she walked to freedom in the year before the abolition of slavery in New York. She was only able to take one with her five children, when she escaped. Isaac and Maria Van Wagener gave her refuge and offered to pay the slave owner 20 dollars for her services until slavery was abolished.

Whilst there, Sojourner discovered her five year old child had been sold illegally to a slave owner in Alabama. With the help of the Van Wageners, she took the case to Court. The case was decided in Soujourner's favour and she became the first person of African American origin to win a justice case against a white slave owner. During this time, she became a strong believer in Christianity. Through her connections with the Church she campaigned for the abolition of slavery.

She became a prominent campaigner for women's rights and racial equality. An extremely strong-willed woman, she changed her slave name, which was Isabella Baumfree, to Soujouner Truth in 1843.

She used her determination to be free of slavery to rise above injustice, improving her own life and the lives of others in the process. Her outstanding speech, later called *Ain't I A Woman*, delivered without notes at the 1851 Women's Convention at Akron, Ohio inspired abolitionists. In the Civil War, she helped recruit African American troops for the Union Army.

Recognition

Although not a dedicated monument to Sojourner, the Broadway United Church of Christ Broadway – previously Broadway Tabernacle - was central to the abolitionist movement in New York. Sojourner spoke at a suffragist convention at the Tabernacle in 1853. The Church has relocated more than once since Truth's day and is now based at 2504 Broadway/93rd Street so the building you see today is not the same place where Sojourner stood up all those years ago. Attend a Sunday service, workshop or discussion group. Alternatively, visit the Church when there is no organised activity, to appreciate the quiet and sanctity of the building and consider the history of social change which this church has been associated with.

The African Burial Ground Monument stands in Lower Manhattan, marking what is believed to have been the burial place for between 15,000 and 20,000 African-American men, women and children. The Monument is a National Historic Monument and National Landmark. The grounds regularly serve as a location for cultural events and exhibitions.

Sojourner is buried at Oak Hill Cemetery, Battle Creek, Michigan, alongside members of her family.

Social Worker and Humanitarian

Caroline Chisholm

Achievements

Born in England, Caroline travelled to Sydney, Australia in 1838 with her husband Captain Chisholm and their two sons. They had lived in Madras, India, for a number of years where Caroline founded the Female School of Industry for Daughters of Soldiers. Caroline recognised the need to educate the young convict women who arrived in Sydney. So she set about establishing the Female Immigrants' Home against much opposition. In all, 96 girls lived there at any one time. Caroline helped them gain employment. Within a year, all the young women had entered into employment. Also, 23 families were settled on land at Roberts Town.

However, Caroline's application for more land was rejected by the government. So she set sail back to England with her family in 1846 to gain political support for immigrants. There, Caroline spoke to the House of Lord's Committee about the issues facing young women and families in Australia. In 1849, the Family Colonisation Loan Society was established. This helped to support the emigration of families to the Australian colonies. The Society was supported by high profile people, such as Charles Dickens. In 1850, Caroline produced a famous pamphlet titled *The A.B.C. of Colonisation.*

The *Caroline Chisholm* was a ship built by ship builder W.S. Lindsay which set sail for Australia in 1853 with many immigrants. Caroline also set sail for Melbourne, Australia in 1854, with her five children. Her husband had gone ahead to Australia three years earlier. On arrival, Caroline found Australia in the grip of gold fever. She travelled to the gold fields to offer assistance to the young women and families living there. Once there, many suggestions were made about how to improve living standards.

In 1857, Caroline was diagnosed with kidney disease. She was weakened, but found time in 1862 to establish a girls' school. After a couple of years, the Chisholm family decided to return to England, which they did in 1866.

Living in Liverpool was a direct contrast to the untamed bushland of Australia. Caroline grew increasingly frail, and passed away in 1877. Her life had been one of adventure and politics. Her dedication to the improvement of living standards and opportunities for young women and families settling in Australia is remembered with gratitude by thousands. She was never deterred from her path by bureaucratic red tape and always fought for what she believed in. She is an inspiration to many.

Recognition

Caroline's portrait, painted by Thomas Fairland in 1852, is held at the National Library of Australia in Canberra. She is described as 'The Emigrant's Friend'. That was inscribed on her headstone. Caroline's face featured on the Australian five dollar note for more than 20 years. She was also featured on the Australian five cent piece for a time. The suburb of Chisholm in Canberra, Australia, is named after Caroline, as is the electorate division of the same name.

She was included in the White Hat 200 Significant Australians. She is commemorated in the Calendar of Saints by the Church of England. There is a movement who believe she should be canonised as a saint by the Catholic Church.

The Caroline Chisholm Library can be found on Lonsdale Street, Melbourne. The Caroline Chisholm Centre is located in Canberra, Australia, and houses several Australian Government services. Several schools in Australia and England are named for Caroline. These include:

- Caroline Chisholm School in Canberra, ACT, Australia
- Caroline Chisholm College in Glenmore Park, NSW, Australia
- Caroline Chisholm Catholic College in Braybrook, VIC, Australia
- The Chisholm Institute of TAFE in Melbourne, VIC, Australia
- Caroline Chisholm School in Wootton Fields, Northampton, England

In 1969, the Caroline Chisholm Society was established in Melbourne, Australia. It offers support for pregnant women and young families. The Caroline Chisholm Education Foundation was established to support vocational education. Many educational grants are available from the Foundation for individuals and organisations.

Caroline was buried with her husband in Billing Road Cemetery in Northampton, England. She had made major contributions to improve the lives of others in Australia, India and Britain.

Women's Rights Activist

Emmeline Pankhurst

Achievements

How could women get equal rights and particularly the right to vote? Emmeline Pankhurst focused on those questions. As one of the important campaigners for women's civil liberties, she actually lost her own liberty on many occasions and was frequently arrested for leading marches and protests.

Public demonstrations were not enough and Emmeline founded the Women's Social and Political Union in 1903. It became a powerful force for change and some of the women became militant and attacked public buildings, staged hunger strikes or set fire to property.

Emmeline was in the front line of the battles, having seen the poverty and distress of women and their families as a Poor Law Guardian. She initially tried to get reform by joining the Labour Party, but was refused membership because she was a woman.

By forming her own organisation, she attracted many women and they showed what people power can do. On 21 June 1908, 500,000 activists rallied in Hyde Park to demand votes for women.

"Deeds," Emmeline wrote, "not words, was to be our permanent motto."

The WSPU, as it was known, was regarded by Emmeline as a political party that had many followers, but no votes and no members of Parliament.

In one sense, it could have been a new civil war, as families were divided. Many arguments broke out between spouses as well as at local and national levels. Only the commencement of the First World War led to the movement abating its action, in order to support the war effort.

It took at long time for women to achieve the vote. By that time, Emmeline was in her later years. Although selected to contest an election for the Conservative Party, she could not be elected to Parliament because of ill health.

Recognition

In the history of Britain, Emmeline Pankhurst's name stands out as a champion of civil liberties. Emmeline led the way in fighting for the rights that modern women now have. She has been commemorated in various ways, including:

- A statue of Emmeline stands outside othe British Parliament, a tribute to her impact on democracy and politics in Britain
- The National Portrait Gallery included a painting of her in 1929

- The BBC dramatised her life in the 1974 mini-series *Shoulder to Shoulder*
- In 1987, one of her homes in Manchester was opened as the Pankhurst Centre, an all-women gathering space and museum

Her contributions as a women's rights activist now form the focus of study for many courses in politics and women studies.

Summary

Reflecting on the achievements of the women in this book, I noted patterns were emerging which may be able to guide future action. It is incredible what these women achieved.

All of them helped build the foundations for modern women to have full lives and contribute in their respective fields. Yet, during their lifetime, they fought against the odds to establish basic rights, which today we may take for granted.

Action Followed Their Heart

Many of the women who made amazing contributions were driven by their beliefs. Indeed, some of them felt that their God was speaking to them directly, telling them what to do.

Florence Nightingale, for example, said that her great work was commanded from above. She wrote, "God spoke to me and called me to his service." It was the start of an amazing career in which she developed the profession of nursing. In so doing, she went beyond beliefs to hard, cold facts. She became a statistician, collecting vital information to show the need for treatment and the results from effective action.

Mother Teresa, at the age of 12, was convinced that she would become a missionary. At the age of 18, she waved goodbye to her family, never to see them again. Her heart told her to join the Catholic Church and serve God. She was a nun for many years, before finding her vocation. She attributed her decision to a direct order from God. "I was to leave the convent to help the poor." Prayer by itself was not enough. Direct action was required.

Not all the women were religious, but they had strong beliefs. Emmeline Pankhurst fought for women's political rights. She came from a well-educated family, but was more motivated by what she saw in the streets.

The poverty and disease and the crippling effect it had on women touched her heart, as much as her head. She used shock and direct-action tactics to bring about change.

No doubt, explanations could be offered about the voices that the women heard, particularly those who said that God had given them an order. It could be said they were deluded, but they went on to create a reality out of their perceptions. The reality in most cases was that they changed the world for the better.

Learning from Action

Few of the women who achieved great things in their lives were educated in the formal sense. Indeed, it was seen as a waste of time to educate young girls, as it was felt they would not need the skills of reading and writing and mathematics. Their place was in the home, bringing up their families and tending to the needs of their breadwinning husbands.

Women who were educated, nevertheless, learnt a great deal from action. In particular, Elizabeth Blackwell made major contributions to improving people's health. She did so by practical means, despite opposition. She set up hospital facilities, particularly for women and children.

Also, in the field of education, Maria Montessori led the way by establishing her 'learning by doing' approach. That was very different to the conventional approach of the time. She placed the emphasis on learning first, rather than teaching.

Other women who achieved greatness did not wait on formal education. In those days, there were no business courses like the MBA degree. Their education came from running a business and reflecting on their successes and failures. As a result, they took action to improve things, rather than just complain.

Name Changes and Brands

Women usually changed their name when they became married. However, it was less common for women to change their name to fit their business role. Those who felt it would advance their efforts did so in the form of taking a *nom de plume*. Today, we refer to it as a brand name to distinguish the product or service it represents.

Coco Chanel changed her first name. Agnese Gonxhe Bojaxhiu was born in

1910. On becoming a nun, she changed her name to Sister Teresa. Later, she was called Mother Teresa for her work with children and the name stuck, reflecting her image and contributions.

Determination to Succeed

The women who achieved great things in their lives were dedicated. Once they identified the direction they wanted to take, they pursued it with great zeal. There was no stopping them, despite many obstacles in their paths.

Elizabeth Blackwell, the first female doctor to qualify in the USA, and the first to be registered in England, had many battles to face. She applied to 17 medical schools. Each one of them rejected her. Only when the students of a college were allowed a vote on entry did she get a place.

This example shows that nothing was given to women at that time. They had to fight for their rights to gain qualifications. Even when qualified, it was hard to get work.

Organisation of People and Resources

The women who made major achievements, in the main, set up organisations to put their ideas into practice. They had to because the organisations of the time were led by men, most of whom were opposed to women 'interfering in their domains.'

Florence Nightingale did not rely on her ideas and prayers alone. She built an organisation to train nurses and carry out research on people's health.

Forceful or Gentle Personalities

It was alleged that women did not have a head for business and politics. Various other assumptions went with this. For example, as women were believed to be the 'fairer sex', it was assumed they did not have the toughness to deal with big issues. It was also assumed that they would not be able to argue with men and get their way on the big decisions. The feeling was that men would speak forcefully and women would back down.

Golda Meir, who became the first female Prime Minister of Israel, was another who changed her name a number of times. She was named Golda Mabovitch at birth and married Morris Meyerson. On emigrating to Israel and becoming involved in politics, she changed her name to Golda Meir on advice from her colleagues. She then became known as the 'Iron Lady', for her resilience and determination to defend the interests of her nation. She did this in Russia, facing up to the communist dictators. Also, she opposed the British. She battled to gain resources from the USA, whilst leading the fight against the Arab countries which attacked Israel.

Likewise, the women who led the suffragette movement to get women the vote were tough and determined. Some, like Emmeline Pankhurst, were imprisoned for their cause. She along with others argued forcefully for change and eventually secured the vote and other rights.

There are many examples of women taking tough decisions to defend and promote their interests. That is increasingly accepted today, but in the early days of the fight for women's rights it was not the case.

Ability to Make Discoveries

Prior to the 20th Century, women did not make many discoveries, because for the most part, they did not travel, nor did they have the opportunity to study new areas. Therefore, an assumption grew that women could not do those kinds of things. It is only in the last 200 years that women have gradually had these opportunities and they have made good use of them.

Marie Curie is celebrated for her scientific discoveries. She is the only woman to have won two Nobel Prizes. Amazing achievements indeed, particularly when she was working in the French language, as she came from Poland. Her research and development abilities were extraordinary and she has become a role model for many women.

Women Who Succeeded In Business

Prior to 1900, few women entered the world of business other than in jobs that were not at the managerial or owner level. Again assumptions were made that women were not born with those gifts and could not learn them.

The trouble with assumptions is that they often become reality, because people then act on them to make them come true. However, some women decided to test the assumptions, not just to prove people wrong, but to make their mark in the world.

Women Overcoming Disabilities

Today, there is a recognition that disabled people need to be given equal opportunities. Laws are passed in many countries to give force to the principles.

However, in days past this was not so. The disabled had little chance of living a reasonable life. Ada Lovelace showed what could be done despite being ill for a period of her life. She went on to make a major contribution to the development of computers.

Other women succeeded despite having severe illness and being deprived of family members through disease. They did not let their disability hold them back.

Women as Pioneers

It is often forgotten how many women have led by being pioneers. They have established the foundations on which communities have developed, providing the family leadership to guide the new generation. These are not always seen as amazing contributions, but in the early days of any community, women who set the foundations were leaders.

One of these was Susannah Holmes. At the age of 17, she was a convict in Norwich Prison, England. Her sentence was to be deported to Australia. After nine months on a convict ship, she arrived with her baby. She married the baby's father, another convict, and became a founding mother of a new country.

In every community, there have been women who have been pioneers. They set the standards. They helped the new generation learn the skills to move forward. They did not always have formal titles or political roles. Their contributions may not be recorded in any book such as this, but they have contributed as much, if not more, than those who are honoured.

Next Phases

The stories of the amazing women in this book show what can be achieved. However, there is still a divide between the opportunities provided for some and the lack of opportunity for others. The battle for women's rights goes on.

It will be interesting to see the new generation of amazing women and what they do. The opportunities are there to be taken. Will it start with a call from God, or a strong feeling based on political beliefs? Or will it be career women who use their skills to make scientific, social and commercial breakthroughs? Will the next frontier for women be in the developing countries where education levels and health levels are below those elsewhere? Or, will the next frontier be in the universities, or business or political organisations? There are more women than ever now engaged outside the home in career activities. There is no doubt that we will see many more amazing women emerge.

Index

Amazing People Team

The following have contributed to the publications of the Amazing People Club for which we express our appreciation.

Frances Corcoran – Vice President - International Publishing

Emily Hamilton - Illustrator

Emma Braithwaite - Publishing Coordinator

Katharine Smith - Managing Editor

Kirri Robinson - Editor

Lisa Moffatt - Editor

James Maxwell - Graphic Designer - Decogekko Creative

Rodney Bain - Creative Project Manager – Varjak Designs

Denis Bedson - Support Illustrator

Monica Lawlor - Publishing Coordinator

Alan Ernst - Guest Editor

Paul Harris - Chief Audio Engineer

Jennifer Harris - Audio Coordinator

James Rix - Audio Engineer

Emily Moxon - Support Editor

Gregory Robinson - Audio Engineer

Dr Charles Margerison - President and Author

The Amazing People Club®

Explore the Amazing People Club Series....

Other exciting books in the series include:

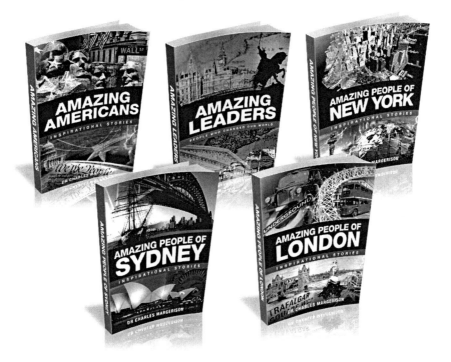

Many of our titles are also available in audio formats:

Amazing People Series:
Amazing Americans
Amazing Women
Amazing Scientists
Amazing Musicians

Amazing City Series:
Amazing People of New York
Amazing People of London
Amazing People of Paris
Amazing People of Sydney

To learn more about our Amazing People Club visit
www.amazingpeopleclub.com

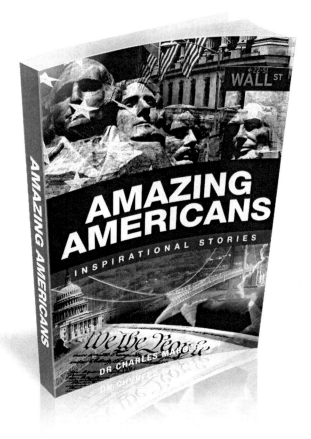

AMAZING AMERICANS

From poverty to riches. From colonists and slaves to citizens with a vote. From a log cabin to the White House. All images of the United States of America.

How did people transform a nation to be a power house of business and democratic life?

Thomas Jefferson and Abraham Lincoln established principles. Within the political frameworks, people like Earhart, Salk, Morse, Julian and Gilbreth changed their nation. Each of the BioViews® provides an insight into their contributions, as if they had been interviewed, but without purporting to use their words. Be inspired by those who made exceptional contributions. Experience these and many other outstanding stories in *Amazing Americans*.